AMAZED BY JESUS

The Big Picture of the Life of Christ

VOLUME 2

MARC HINDS

Amazed By Jesus: The Big Picture of the Life of Christ (Volume 2)

Published by 21st Century Christian
2809 12th Avenue South
Nashville, Tennessee 37204

Printed in the United States of America.

LCCN: 2019917025
ISBN-13: 978-0-89-098852-7

Italics within Scripture quotations indicate emphasis added.

Interior design, typesetting and cover by Hinds Design (www.HindsDesign.com).
Cover image: Vincent van Gogh's "The Good Samaritan (after Delacroix)," 1890.

Hinds, Marc.
Amazed by Jesus : the big picture of the life of Christ / Marc Hinds.

CONTENTS

Artist's rendering of Jesus' tomb

FIGURES

MAPS

Map 11 © Marc Hinds (**www.hindsdesign.com**).
Maps 12–15 © ESV Study Bible (**www.crossway.com**).

ARTWORK

PHOTOS

ABBREVIATIONS

Old Testament

Gen	Genesis	Song	Song of Solomon
Ex	Exodus	Isa	Isaiah
Lev	Leviticus	Jer	Jeremiah
Num	Numbers	Lam	Lamentations
Deut	Deuteronomy	Ezek	Ezekiel
Josh	Joshua	Dan	Daniel
Judg	Judges	Hos	Hosea
Ruth	Ruth	Joel	Joel
1–2 Sam	1–2 Samuel	Amos	Amos
1–2 Kgs	1–2 Kings	Obad	Obadiah
1–2 Chron	1–2 Chronicles	Jonah	Jonah
Ezra	Ezra	Mic	Micah
Neh	Nehemiah	Nah	Nahum
Esth	Esther	Hab	Habakkuk
Job	Job	Zeph	Zephaniah
Ps(s)	Psalm(s)	Hag	Haggai
Prov	Proverbs	Zech	Zechariah
Eccl	Ecclesiastes	Mal	Malachi

New Testament

Matt	Matthew	1–2 Thess	1–2 Thessalonians
Mark	Mark	1–2 Tim	1–2 Timothy
Luke	Luke	Titus	Titus
John	John	Phlm	Philemon
Acts	Acts	Heb	Hebrews
Rom	Romans	James	James
1–2 Cor	1–2 Corinthians	1–2 Pet	1–2 Peter
Gal	Galatians	1–3 John	1–3 John
Eph	Ephesians	Jude	Jude
Phil	Philippians	Rev	Revelation
Col	Colossians		

Josephus

Ant.	Josephus, *Jewish Antiquities*
J.W.	Josephus, *Jewish War*

ANALYTICAL OUTLINE FOR *AMAZED BY JESUS*

MINISTRY OF JESUS CHRIST (CONTINUED FROM VOLUME 1)

Palestine in the Time of Jesus
Antipas
Philip
Archelaus
SYRIA
Mt. Hermon
Caesarea Philippi
Tyre
Phoenicia
LAKE HULAH
Trachonitis
Ptolemais
GALILEE
Bethsaida
Capernaum
SEA OF GALILEE
Cana
Sepphoris
Hippus
Mt. Carmel
Nazareth
Mt. Tabor
Bethany beyond the Jordan (north location)
MEDITERRANEAN SEA
Jordan River
DECAPOLIS
Caesarea
Scythopolis (Bethshan)
Baptismal site
SAMARIA
Salim
Aenon
Gerasa (Jerash)
Sebaste (Samaria)
Sychar (Shechem)
Joppa
PEREA
Philadelphia (Rabbath Ammon)
Bethany beyond the Jordan (Bethabara)
Jamnia
Jericho
Jerusalem
Bethany
NABATEA
Ashkelon
Bethlehem
Qumran
JUDEA
Herodium
DEAD SEA
N
Hebron
Machaerus
Gaza
Scale
0
10
20
30 mi
IDUMEA
Masada

LESSON 10

Later Judean Ministry (#96–111)

Luke 10:1–13:21
John 7:11–10:39

In a little over six months, Jesus would be murdered. During his three-month Later Judean Ministry (Lesson 10), he stayed close to Jerusalem and had several heated run-ins with the religious leaders. As their resentment toward him grew, the religious leaders attempted to kill Jesus—twice. These explosive encounters compelled him to leave the region and head east across the Jordan River into Perea for a few months (Lesson 11). He would return in mid-April for the Passover, one final time (Figure 48).

The Last Months of Jesus' Life

Ministry	Timeframe	Lesson	Feast Marker	Sections
Later Judean Ministry	Three months (Oct–Dec A.D. 29)	Lesson 10	Beginning of the Feast of Tabernacles	#96–111
Perean Ministry	Three and a half months (Jan–mid-April A.D. 30)	Lesson 11	After the Feast of Dedication (Hanukkah) until Passover	#112–127
The Final Week	One week (mid-April A.D. 30)	Lessons 12–14	Start of Passover	#128–168
Resurrection and Post-Resurrection Appearances	Forty days (Acts 1:3; mid-May A.D. 30)	Lesson 15	Ten days before Pentecost	#169–184

Figure 48.

Jesus at the Feast of Tabernacles (#96–99)

John 7:11–8:59

It was now early October of A.D. 29. The people had gathered in Jerusalem for the annual Feast of Tabernacles, a popular week-long holiday that commemorated the 40-year wilderness wanderings of ancient Israel. They also celebrated the fruit harvest of produce such as grapes, figs, pomegranates, and olives.

Mixed Reaction to Jesus (#96)

John 7:11–52

Some of the people were confused about Jesus. On the one hand, they knew the religious leaders were antagonistic toward him. Yet, they hadn't arrested him. This made the people wonder if maybe the religious leaders secretly believed him to be the Messiah after all.

During this celebratory time, many of the people were looking for Jesus, hoping to see and hear him. A few days into the week-long feast, they got their wish. Jesus began to publicly teach in the temple. As the people listened to him, the crowds were amazed by Jesus' ability to speak so effectively (cf. Acts 4:13). He impressed them with his authoritative teaching.

As part of the observance of Sukkoth (Feast of Tabernacles), modern Hebrews temporarily live in make-shift booths to commemorate the ancient Israelites' wilderness wanderings.

But not everyone was convinced. Because of their preconceived notions about the Messiah, many rejected Jesus. Others were unable to accept him because he had previously healed on the Sabbath. Jesus tried to reason with them, explaining that "work" was sometimes performed on the Sabbath, such as the circumcision of male babies whose eighth day of life fell on the Sabbath (cf. Lev 12:3). And so, they should not condemn him for "working" on the Sabbath, but rather celebrate his acts of healing.

Near the end of the Feast of Tabernacles, the priest would take water from the pool of Siloam and carry it in a golden pitcher to the altar. This was accompanied by great celebration, including trumpets blowing and people shouting. The celebration culminated with the pouring out of the water. Although not recorded in the Old Testament, this tradition was part of the commemoration of God's provision of water for the people during the wilderness wanderings.

This beautiful ceremony served as the background for Jesus' teaching about "living water."

> On the last day of the feast, the great day, Jesus stood up and cried out, "If anyone thirsts, let him come to me and drink. Whoever believes in me, as the Scripture has said, 'Out of his heart will flow rivers of living water' " (John 7:37–38).

Jesus was claiming to bring people spiritual refreshment (cf. John 4:14). Having earlier identified himself with the manna in the wilderness (John 6:35), he did the same with the miraculous provision of water. Jesus was claiming to be the source of new life.

The age of the Messiah was upon them. Why wouldn't they believe in him?

The Woman Caught in Adultery (#97)

John 7:53–8:11

In your copy of the Bible, the passage in John 7:53–8:11 about the woman caught in adultery is probably bracketed. Although there is some evidence for its authenticity, the earliest copies of the Gospel of John do not include them. These manuscripts were not available in the 17th century when the King James Version was translated.

It is a beautiful story about Jesus' compassion and forgiveness, which would help explain why these 12 verses were preserved by enough copyists of the New Testament. In fact, many Christians today believe this event could have happened, since the incident is consistent with what is taught elsewhere in the Scriptures.

According to John 7:53–8:11, Jesus was teaching in the temple when he was suddenly interrupted by the scribes and Pharisees. They brought before him a woman who had been caught in the act of sexual immorality, a sin publishable by stoning (Lev 20:10). They used this woman to test and potentially embarrass Jesus. If he forgave the woman outright, he would lose respect with the people. If Jesus condemned her to death, the Romans would likely descend upon him and arrest him.

Jesus was not startled or worried. In fact, he seemingly ignored them as he bent down and began writing on the ground with his finger. The scribes and Pharisees continued to pepper him with questions, but Jesus did not acknowledge them. At last, he stood up and spoke.

> "Let him who is without sin among you be the first to throw a stone at her" (John 8:7).

And then, Jesus bent down again and resumed writing on the ground with his finger.

The religious leaders failed in their effort to embarrass him. Instead, they were the ones who left in shame. One by one, the religious leaders filed out, leaving only Jesus and the woman. Although he most certainly did not approve of her sinful behavior, Jesus had shown her compassion and forgiveness. "Go and from now on sin no more," he told her.

John 8:12–20 "I Am the Light of the World" (#98)

The Feast of Tabernacles is a festival of water and lights. Jesus said earlier that "rivers of living water" will flow from the Messiah's "belly" to quench the spiritual thirst of the believer (John 7:38). It should come as no surprise when he also talks about lights.

A young priest climbs a ladder to reach one of the four lamps in the Court of the Women in order to fill them with oil.

At night during the festival, four extremely large lampstands on top of massive towers were lit up in the Court of the Women, bathing the entire temple grounds with brilliant light. This display of light symbolized God's powerful presence during the wilderness wanderings as he traveled with the Israelites (Ex 13:21).

With this backdrop, Jesus declared, "I am the light of the world." Because God's presence was in the pillar of fire, Jesus was making a lofty claim about himself. Additionally, God had spoken through his Old Testament prophets, anticipating a future time when "the LORD will be your everlasting light" (Isa 60:19). Jesus was now claiming to be this light—but not just for Israel.

> Again Jesus spoke to them, saying, "I am the light of the world. Whoever follows me will not walk in darkness, but will have the light of life" (John 8:12).

Jesus' Relationship to God the Father (#99a)

John 8:21–30

The religious leaders balked at this self-assertion. A heated discussion ensued, but not over light. It's about parentage; specifically, who was Jesus' father and who was their father. The question of parentage became a topic when Jesus claimed that all he was doing was the will of his Father who sent him.

The religious leaders, of course, rejected the idea that Jesus was the Son of God. But Jesus continued to press them. They must believe in him, he warned.

> "I told you that you would die in your sins, for unless you believe that I am he you will die in your sins" (John 8:24).

In response to this incredible claim, they asked him, "Who are you?" They couldn't believe someone would talk like this about himself. Jesus then made reference to his crucifixion and exaltation.

> "When you have lifted up the Son of Man, then you will know that I am he, and that I do nothing on my own authority, but speak just as the Father taught me" (John 8:28).*

Jesus knew these are the very people who would be directly responsible for his death on the cross. And yet, he loved them and wanted them to be saved. Some of them do believe (v. 30), but their faith was short-lived: They simply couldn't accept that Jesus was the Christ, the Son of God.

"Before Abraham Was, I Am" (#99b)

John 8:31–59

The religious leaders also struggled to believe that God would reject them. After all, they were descendants of Abraham. How was it possible they would die in their sins? Jesus corrected them by telling them who their real father was.

> "You are of your father the devil, and your will is to do your father's desires. He was a murderer from the beginning, and does not stand in the truth, because there is no truth in him. When he lies, he speaks out of his own character, for he is a liar and the father of lies" (John 8:44).

---

* Jesus described himself as the Son of Man who will be "lifted up" three times in John's Gospel (John 3:14, #32b; 8:28, #99a; 12:32–34, #130a). See especially the discussion on page 95.

The Great "I AM"

God said to Moses, "I AM WHO I AM. . . . Say this to the people of Israel: 'I AM has sent me to you.' "
—Ex 3:14

"I am the Alpha and the Omega," says the Lord God, "who is and who was and who is to come, the Almighty."
—Rev 1:8

God, Jesus, and the Holy Spirit are eternal. They have no beginning or end.

This power is hard to describe, but extremely important to comprehend.

Also prominent in this heated exchange was the concept of truth. Jesus said that anyone who believed in him "will know the truth, and the truth will set you free" (John 8:32). The religious leaders failed to understand how they were in bondage to sin and that Jesus could lead them to freedom: "If the Son sets you free, then you will be free indeed," he added.

Throughout his discussion with the religious leaders, Jesus made an assertion about himself several times, using the words, "I am..." (John 8:12, 24, 28). These were veiled references to the "I AM" declaration God made in Ex 3:14.* In this passage, God revealed that "I AM" is his personal name. As a name, "I AM" represents God's eternal nature and omnipotence. Here at the end of his exhange with them, Jesus took on this name as a self-assertion when he said, "Before Abraham was, *I am*" (John 8:58).

> "Your father Abraham rejoiced that he would see my day. He saw it and was glad." So the Jews said to him, "You are not yet fifty years old, and have you seen Abraham?" Jesus said to them, "Truly, truly, I say to you, before Abraham was, I am" (John 8:58).

They understood exactly what Jesus was saying. Jesus did not say, "Before Abraham was, *I became*," but "I am." He was claiming to be preexistent, just like God the Father. Such "blasphemy" was more than they could stand. In their righteous indignation, they started gathering stones to throw at Jesus, just as the Law of Moses prescribed (Lev 24:16). But Jesus slipped away from their sight and hid from them (cf. Luke 4:30, #39).

During what was supposed to be a time of celebration and feasting, the Jewish leaders had murder in their hearts. They would, as a matter of fact, attempt to stone Jesus again at the next feast in Jerusalem, which is the Feast of Dedication (John 10:31, #111). For now, Jesus left Jerusalem and continued his Judean Ministry elsewhere.

---

* In the Old Testament, the personal name of God is used nearly 7,000 times. Normally translated as "the LORD," it is derived from the verb, "to be" or "I am."

Rearrangement of #100–101

John 9:1–10:21

In piecing together the chronology of Jesus' ministry across all four Gospels, it seems that the events of John 9:1–10:21 (#100–101) do not occur during the Feast of Tabernacles, as do the events recorded in John 7:11–8:59 (#96–99). Rather, the healing of the blind man (John 9, #100) and the "Good Shepherd" discourse (John 10:1–21, #101) likely happened three months later during the Feast of Dedication, placing them between #110 and #111 (see Figure 49). This deviation from A. T. Robertson's *Harmony of the Gospels* is based on the following observations:

1. At the end of John 8 (#99b), the religious leaders attempted to stone Jesus to death. Although they would again become enraged at him and attempt to stone him later during the eight-day Feast of Dedication (John 10:31, #111), the tone of John 9:1–10:21 (#100–101) does not seem to indicate such a high level of antagonism. Three months between public appearances would help explain this difference.
2. John 10:22–39 (#111) definitely occurred during the Feast of Dedication, as indicated by v. 22. The connector "at that time" in v. 22 closely links John 9:1–10:21 (#100–101) with these events (#111). Also, the analogy of the shepherd and the sheep in John 10:1–18 (#101) is resumed in John 10:22–29 (#111), further linking these two sections together.
3. In both John 8:12 (#98) and John 9:5 (#100), Jesus said, "I am the light of the world." The Feast of Tabernacles included a celebration involving the lighting of the menorah, making this an appropriate background for such a statement (see page 4). The Feast of Dedication also did, making it an equally appropriate occasion (see page 19 of volume 1 and page 17 of volume 2). It seems, then, that the healing of the blind man fits neatly between these two festivals that involve lights.

Later Judean Ministry Rearranged (#96–111)

Occasion	Citation	Passage	Section
The Feast of Tabernacles	Jerusalem	John 7:11–8:59	#96–99
Luke's Central Section (beginning)	Probably in Judea	Luke 10:1–13:21	#102–110
The Feast of Dedication, on the Sabbath	**Jerusalem**	**John 9:1–10:21**	**#100–101**
The Feast of Dedication, soon afterward	Jerusalem	John 10:22–39	#111

Figure 49.

Luke 10:1–13:21

Luke's Central Section Begins (#102–110)

Luke 9:51–19:44 are often referred to as Luke's Central Section. Chronologically, these events took place at the end of the Galilean Ministry (Lesson 9, #93) and continued until the start of the Final Week (Lesson 12, #128). The Central Section covers the last few months of Jesus' ministry before his arrival in Jerusalem.

Much of this material is unique to Luke, including numerous parables (Parables 16–31 and 33; Parables 9–10 are repeated in #110; see pages 144–145 of volume 1). Various themes emerge in them.

Themes in Luke's Central Section

Theme	Citation
The kingdom of God is coming	Luke 9:60; 10:9; 16:16
The cost and benefits of true discipleship	Luke 9:57–62; 12:4–12; 13:24; 14:25–34
The necessity of prayer	Luke 11:1–13; 18:1–14
True repentance	Luke 13:1–5; 15:1–32; 16:30
The importance of genuine faith	Luke 12:28; 17:5–6; 18:1–8
The proper use of possessions	Luke 16:1–31
The necessity of suffering	Luke 10:1–9

Figure 50.

Another prominent theme in this section is Jesus' focus on making his way toward Jerusalem, the place of his impending death.

> When the days drew near for him to be taken up, he set his face to go to Jerusalem (Luke 9:51; see also Luke 13:22, 33; 17:11; 19:4).

The phrase, "he set his face" (Luke 9:51, 53) is a Jewish expression that denotes Jesus' determination to fulfill his mission. Nothing would deter him from going to Jerusalem and dying for the sins of humanity.

The events of Luke 10:1–13:21 (#102–110) likely occurred in November and early December of A.D. 29 between the Feasts of Tabernacles and Dedication. During these weeks, Jesus focused on his disciples, preparing them for when they are without him. He also interacted with many others who were not yet his disciples.

The "Way"

[Jesus] went on his **way** through towns and villages, teaching and journeying toward Jerusalem.

—Luke 13:22

The simple word *way* becomes theologically significant in Luke's Central Section. (Also read Luke 13:33; 17:11; 19:4.)

In the book of Acts, Christianity and its followers are called the "way" (Acts 9:2; 19:9; 22:4).

The Seventy (#102)

Luke 10:1–24

During the Galilean Ministry, Jesus sent his 12 apostles out in pairs to preach and perform miracles in Galilee (#70b). He now sent them into Judea as part of a group of 70 disciples.*

As before, they were expected to pack lightly, so they would be prepared to move quickly from village to village. The scant provisions also helped these itinerant preachers to develop stronger trust in God. They would be relying on him to provide for them through the generosity of others along the way.

Many gladly welcomed these representatives of the Messiah. When they entered a home, the apostles and the 70 were instructed to say, "Peace to this house!" When "a son of peace" responded favorably, they should stay. Otherwise, they should move on to others who were interested in hearing the gospel.

The rejection of the message was also emphasized in Jesus' instructions. As he did when he sent the apostles out in Galilee, Jesus bemoaned the faithlessness of the people who lived in the Galilean cities of Chorazin and Bethsaida (#58). Despite seeing many miracles, they had rejected Jesus. These laments were repeated as Jesus anticipated widespread rejection of the gospel.

When they returned, the 70 reported how successful they had been in their preaching efforts. When they told him they were able to cast out demons, Jesus responded by saying, "I saw Satan fall like lightning from heaven." The devil's stranglehold on the world was starting to loosen.

Then Jesus told them the real reason they should be so excited.

> "Do not rejoice in this, that the spirits are subject to you, but rejoice that your names are written in heaven" (Luke 10:20).

---

* There is a textual variant that reads 72 (ESV, NIV, NLT). The Thomas and Gundry *Harmony* prefers 70 (NASB, KJV, NKJV), which corresponds with the number of 70 elders that Moses appointed to help him in his ministry (Num 11:24–25). In a similar way, Jesus—the second Moses—is commissioning his ministry assistants, too.

The religious leaders should have been the ones to accept Jesus. Instead, ordinary folks, represented in the number of the 70, were the people who gladly accepted Jesus as the Messiah and carried his message.

> Then turning to the disciples he said privately, "Blessed are the eyes that see what you see! For I tell you that many prophets and kings desired to see what you see, and did not see it, and to hear what you hear, and did not hear it" (Luke 10:23–24).

Their success in the mission field pointed to the future when the gospel would be carried to the entire world by ordinary disciples.

Luke 10:25–37

Story of the Good Samaritan (#103)

Throughout Luke's Central Section, Jesus was approached by various people who engaged him in conversation. Sometimes, they asked from pure motives. But whenever a trained professional or religious leader asked Jesus a question, normally it was to challenge him, to test him or to embarrass him. Jesus always turned the tables on those who asked these sorts of questions.

This time, it was a lawyer, an expert in the law of Moses. "Teacher, what shall I do to inherit eternal life?" he asked Jesus. As he often did, Jesus answered the question with a question.

> [Jesus] said to him, "What is written in the Law? How do you read it?" And [the lawyer] answered, "You shall love the Lord your God with all your heart and with all your soul and with all your strength and with all your mind, and your neighbor as yourself." And he said to him, "You have answered correctly; do this, and you will live" (Luke 10:26–28).

The lawyer quoted Deut 6:5 and Lev 19:18, two important Old Testament passages that talk about our love for God and our love for others. Pressing Jesus further, the lawyer asked, "Who is my neighbor?" Jesus answered him with the parable of the Good Samaritan.

In this parable, Jesus presented a real-life scenario of a Jewish traveler who was assaulted along the 17-mile stretch of highway from Jericho to Jerusalem.

Robbed and beaten, the traveler was lying half-dead in the road. A priest happened to be traveling that way, too. But instead of stopping to help, the priest avoided him and kept making his way down the road. This course of action was repeated when a Levite, another well-respected member of the Jewish community, came upon the hurt man. All three men—the priest, the Levite and the man left for dead—were Jews. Even though they were his "neighbor," the priest and Levite did nothing to help.

PARABLE 18
The Good Samaritan

Jesus then tells of a third traveler. He wasn't this man's fellow countryman, but a Samaritan. And, he unexpectedly became the hero of the story. Filled with compassion, the Samaritan went to work on the man's wounds, treating them with oil and wine. He hoisted him up on his own beast of burden and took him to a local inn. Taking money from his own pocket, the Samaritan paid for the care of this injured Jewish man he found on the road.

Having concluded the parable, Jesus then asked the lawyer, "Which of these three, do you think, proved to be a neighbor to the man who fell among the robbers?" The lawyer, not able to speak the word *Samaritan*, answered, "The one who showed him mercy." Jesus said to him, "Go and do likewise."

Jesus never really answered the lawyer's question, "Who is my neighbor?" Instead, Jesus turned the situation around by answering a slightly different question: "What kind of a neighbor are you going to be?" Being a "neighbor" means doing what you can with what you have, where you are right now.

Jesus' Visit with Mary and Martha (#104)

Luke 10:38–42

The laywer had quoted two fundamental Old Testament passages. The parable about the neighborly Samaritan had focused on the second of these, "Love your neighbor as yourself." But immediately afterward, Luke's Gospel records an incident involving Jesus' friends, Mary and Martha, that addresses the first Old Testament passage the lawyer quoted about loving God.

When in Bethany, Jesus always enjoyed the company of these sisters and their brother, Lazarus (who is not named here). While hosting a meal in their home, Martha found herself alone in the kitchen, doing what the women typically did. But her sister, Mary, was doing what men typically did: She was sitting at Jesus' feet, listening to him teach.

Martha was none too pleased and asked Jesus to tell Mary to come help her. But instead of rebuking Mary, Jesus rebuked Martha.

> "Martha, Martha, you are anxious and troubled about many things, but one thing is necessary. Mary has chosen the good portion, which will not be taken away from her" (Luke 10:41–42).

In his gentle but firm response to Martha, Jesus emphasized the importance of putting God first in our lives. Other matters are important, but the spiritual always trumps everything else.

Luke 11:1–13

The Need for Persistence in Prayer (#105)

Jesus prayed frequently (Figure 51), making a strong impression on his disciples, who asked him to teach them to pray. John the Baptist, after all, had taught his disciples to pray. In response, Jesus provided them with a model prayer (Luke 11:2–4; cf. Matt 6:9–13, #54f).

The Prayer Life of Jesus

Occasion of Jesus' Prayer	Citation
When baptized, Jesus prayed	Luke 3:21
Jesus often withdrew from others to pray	Luke 5:16
Jesus spent all night in prayer	Luke 6:12
He went to a mountain to pray (and was then transfigured)	Luke 9:28
Jesus is prodded to teach about prayer after his disciples see him praying	Luke 11:1
Jesus prays as he gives thanks for the bread and the cup during the Lord's Supper	Luke 22:17, 19
Jesus tells Peter that he is praying for him	Luke 22:32
Jesus prays in the Garden of Gethsemane	Luke 22:41
Jesus prayed from the cross	Luke 23:34

Figure 51.

He then used this occasion to teach on the importance of praying persistently. A friend inconvenienced his neighbor by knocking on his door late at night asking for help. He was reluctant to answer because everyone was already settled for the night. But because the intruder was persistent and kept knocking, the neighbor finally got out of his bed.

PARABLE 19
A Friend in Need

In sharp contrast to that scenario, we serve a gracious God who wants us to come to him in prayer at any time. He listens to the prayers of his children and is abundant in his blessings, giving us more than just what we need (James 1:5).

Jesus and Beelzebul (#106)

Luke 11:14–36

Because the miracles of Jesus were undeniable, some questioned his power's source. When he cast a demon out of a mute man, Jesus was accused of aligning himself with Satan (see also #61 and #68). "How else could he cast out demons?" they reasoned.

A similar situation occurred a year earlier during Jesus' Galilean Ministry (Matt 12:24, #61). In his response, Jesus proceeded to explain that expulsion of the demon proved "the kingdom of God has come upon you." Jesus further explained that, unless someone filled the void left by the demon, then it would return with "seven other spirits more evil than itself." In other words, the exorcism was only the beginning of the new life.

MIRACLE 29 (see Sec. 68)
Curing a Demon-Possessed Mute Man

As the crowd grew, Jesus turned his attention to the religious leaders. He rebuked them for their refusal to acknowledge him as the Christ by praising the faith of Gentiles in the Old Testament. The city of Nineveh repented at the preaching of Jonah and the queen of Sheba acknowledged the wisdom of Solomon. "And behold, something greater than Solomon is here," Jesus said, referring to himself.

"Woes" on the Pharisees and Scribes (#107)

Luke 11:37–54

When a Pharisee invited Jesus to his home for a meal, he accepted. The legalistic host was startled when he noticed that Jesus did not observe the hand washing ritual of the Pharisees. Jesus used this as an occasion to teach about inward purity.

In a series of scathing woes against the Pharisees, Jesus pointed out their hypocrisy. Outwardly, they may appear holy and righteous when giving alms or tithing. But, they were putting on a show only because they wanted to be admired for their acts of service.

When a lawyer present at the meal told Jesus he was insulting the Pharisees with his words, Jesus turned his attention to lawyers. "Woe to you!" he exclaimed, condemning them for rejecting him as the Messiah and trying to prevent others from accessing him.

Throughout the remainder of his ministry, Jesus continued to be pursued by the religious leaders. Several times, they sent groups to test him. This was especially true whenever he found himself near or in Jerusalem. They simply could not tolerate this pest who made such lofty claims about himself, insulted them by pointing out their shortcomings, and threatened to disrupt their way of life.

Luke 12:1–59

Various Warnings (#108)

During his ministry in Judea, Jesus was greeted by large crowds, much to the dismay of the Pharisees. Having caught the imagination of the people, Jesus continued to point out the hypocrisy of these men as he issued a series of warnings (Figure 52).

Jesus' Various Warnings in Luke 12:1–59

Warning	Citation
Warning the disciples about hypocrisy	Luke 12:1–12
Warning about greed and trust in wealth	Luke 12:13–34
Warning against being unprepared for the Son of Man's coming	Luke 12:35–48
Warning about the coming division	Luke 12:49–53
Warning against failing to discern the present time	Luke 12:54–59

Figure 52.

During one of these exchanges, someone in the audience asked Jesus to help him with a family dispute over his inheritance. Jesus, refusing to get involved, told a parable to counter greed and trust in wealth (Luke 12:16–21). In this parable, a farmer who had an enormously successful crop decided to tear down his barns and build larger ones. He planned to retire early so he could spend his riches on himself. In this famous parable, Jesus called the man a fool because he was not rich toward God. Instead, the man died, leaving his wealth behind.

PARABLE 20
The Rich Fool

In the parable of the Watchful Servants (Luke 12:35–40), Jesus taught about the importance of always being prepared for "the coming of the Son of Man." When all we do is pursue worthless and selfish goals in life, we help no one, including ourselves.

PARABLE 21
The Watchful Servants

In response to his powerful teaching, Jesus was asked by Peter, "Lord, are you telling this parable for us or for all?" The correct answer, of course, was "for all." All people need to prepare their hearts, lest they lose everything in the final judgment.

By way of illustration, Jesus then told a third parable. The Faithful Servant and the Evil Servant (Luke 12:42–48) display two different responses to God's coming judgment. Those who live without regard for the future will suffer the consequences of their sinful neglect. The "faithful and wise" will be rewarded.

PARABLE 22
The Faithful Servant and the Evil Servant

Two Alternatives: Repent or Perish (#109)

Luke 13:1–9

Having listened to Jesus teach about the consequences of sin, several people in the crowd asked him about a recent tragedy. Some Galileans who brought sacrifices to Jerusalem were murdered by Pontius Pilate, the governor of Judea. Their question was, "Do you think these Galileans were worse sinners than all the other Galileans, because they suffered in this way?"

Instead of answering their question, Jesus taught on repentance and the importance of always being ready: "No, I tell you; but unless you repent, you will all likewise perish" (Luke 13:3). Death is inevitable. And so, it doesn't really matter how we die. What's really important is how we live.

Jesus then gave his own illustration. Recently, also in Jerusalem, a tower at Siloam had fallen, killing 18 people.

> "Those eighteen on whom the tower in Siloam fell and killed them: do you think that they were worse offenders than all the others who lived in Jerusalem? No, I tell you; but unless you repent, you will all likewise perish" (Luke 13:4–5).

PARABLE 23
The Barren Fig Tree

Jesus then turned his attention to all of Israel. In the parable of the Barren Fig Tree (Luke 13:6–9), the nation was compared to a fig tree that failed to produce any fruit for a three-year period (cf. Parable 39, #132). In the parable, the vinedresser pleaded with the owner to give the tree one more year before taking drastic measures. He promised to fertilize it and give it special care. "Then if it should bear fruit next year, well and good; but if not, you can cut it down."

Israel had been blessed with the presence of Jesus for three years.* But as a nation, it had not accepted him. Rather, its leaders actively persecuted Jesus and attempted to undermine his teachings at every opportunity.

Soon, this conflict would come to a head. In just a few months, Jesus would be killed at the behest of the Jews during the Passover.

Luke 13:10–21

MIRACLE 30
Healing the Infirm, Bent Woman

Opposition for Healing on the Sabbath (#110)

While teaching in a synagogue on the Sabbath, Jesus healed a woman who had lived for 18 years with a severely bent back. Her deformity was so serious, she could not even stand upright. After witnessing the healing, the synagogue leader complained that Jesus had helped this woman on the Sabbath.

Jesus responded to the man's coldhearted criticism:

> "You hypocrites! Does not each of you on the Sabbath untie his ox or his donkey from the manger and lead it away to water it? And ought not this woman, a daughter of Abraham whom Satan bound for eighteen years, be loosed from this bond on the Sabbath day?" (Luke 13:15–16).

* Jesus is in the third year of his ministry, making it tempting to suggest that he is referring to Israel's rejection of him during this time. The Synoptic Gospels, however, do not indicate the length of his ministry. We know it was over three years because of John's references to several Passover celebrations (see Figure 12, volume 1, pages 32–33).

The common people who were also attending the synagogue service that Sabbath day responded quite differently: they rejoiced. Jesus then told two parables about the kingdom of God and its humble beginnings. They are repeated from Jesus' earlier Galilean ministry (Parables 10–11, #64e and #64f), but they especially were appropriate here during this Sabbath service.

PARABLE 10 (see Sec. 64e)
The Mustard Seed

PARABLE 11 (see Sec. 64f)
The Leaven

- The tiny mustard seed grows into a very large tree.
- The leaven hidden in the bread dough helps produce numerous loaves of bread.

In a similar way, the healing of a crippled woman foreshadowed the ultimate redemptive healing that will affect the entire world and its ailment of sin. The synagogue leader might not have cared much about this infirmed woman. But Jesus did. And the people saw his deep concern for the less fortunate and rejoiced.

Jesus at the Feast of Dedication (#100–101, 111)

John 9:1–10:39

The Feast of Dedication is better known as Hanukkah, which means "dedication." Hanukkah is an eight-day celebration of the nation's successful revolt led by the Maccabees against Syrian oppression and is still observed by Israelis today. First celebrated in 165 B.C., the Feast of Dedication is closely associated with the lighting of the menorah and is often called the Festival of Lights.

Three months earlier, during the Feast of Tabernacles, Jesus had said, "I am the light of the world" (John 8:12, #98). He said it again during the Feast of Dedication (John 9:5). And he proved his claim to be the light by restoring the sight of a man born blind.

Healing of a Man Born Blind (#100)

John 9:1–41

While at the temple on the Sabbath day, Jesus and his disciples saw this man who had been born blind. Relegated to a life of begging, the blind man and others like him typically sat at the gates of the temple as people took pity on them and gave them money (Acts 3:2). But today, Jesus gave him the gift of sight.

Jesus started the healing process by spitting on the ground, making mud with the saliva and then anointing the man's eyes with the mud. Jesus then commanded him to wash off the mud in the

MIRACLE 31
Healing the Man Born Blind

Steps leading to the Pool of Siloam (discovered in 2004).

nearby pool of Siloam, less than a mile away.* The blind man went to the pool still unable to see, but when he returned after washing his eyes, he was able to see.

But he didn't see Jesus. He and his disciples had perhaps gone inside the temple. Jesus would come and find the formerly blind man later (v. 35). In the meantime, this man's faith grew exponentially as he began not only to see physically, but also to perceive spiritually (Figure 53).

Others observed that the blind man could now see. They couldn't believe it. In fact, some said that he must be someone else who only resembled the blind man. As they keep talking about him, he kept saying to them, "I am" (v. 9), identifying Jesus as the one who healed him.

The Growing Faith of the Blind Man

Action Taken	Citation
Takes Jesus at his word and washes his eyes in the pool of Siloam	v. 7
Refers to Jesus as "the man called Jesus"	v. 11
Says that Jesus is a "prophet"	v. 17
Denies that Jesus could be a "sinner"	v. 25
Proclaims that Jesus is "from God"	v. 33
Declares his faith in Jesus and worships him	v. 38

Figure 53.

The Pharisees began their own interrogation of the man. Instead of rejoicing that this blind beggar could now see, the Pharisees were angry with Jesus for healing on the Sabbath. But instead of siding with them, the formerly blind man defended Jesus.

> "Why, this is an amazing thing! You do not know where he comes from, and yet he opened my eyes. We know that God does not listen to sinners, but if anyone is a worshiper of God and does his will, God listens to him. . . . If this man were not from God, he could do nothing" (John 9:30–33).

* Interestingly, the name of this pool, "Siloam," means "sent."

Because he had allied himself with Jesus, the man was soundly rejected by the Pharisees. They expelled him from synagogue worship. It was then that Jesus came and found him (v. 35). By now, his spiritual sight was nearly complete. Jesus asks him, "Do you believe in the Son of Man?" Free from the shackles of the religious leaders, he openly confessed, "Lord, I believe." And then, he worshipped Jesus.

The blind man could now see physically and spiritually. The religious leaders, however, could see physically but not perceive spiritually. They refused to accept that Jesus was the Messiah. He had just restored the eyesight of a man born blind, which was one of the miracles that was supposed to occur in the age of the Messiah (Isa 29:18; 35:5; 42:7). But they were willfully blind to what was right in front of them.

The pool of Siloam served as one of the water reservoirs of Jerusalem. It was surrounded by five porticoes.

"I Am the Good Shepherd" (#101a)

John 10:1–18

Jesus continued to address the blindness of the Pharisees by comparing the kingdom of God to a sheepfold. During the day, sheep were led to a walled pen to sleep in during the night. Sometimes, shepherds combined their flocks, so they could share the responsibility of protecting them. Because sheep recognize the distinctive voice of their shepherd, they would follow him only when he returned in the morning.

Sheep are completely dependent on their shepherd for protection (cf. 1 Sam 17:34–37). In an effort to keep them safe, modern shepherds sleep through the night often at the one and only entrance, adding a layer of security. With the entrance guarded by the shepherd, predators and thieves have to try and climb over the wall to ravage the sheep.

Throughout the Old Testament, God was described as the shepherd of his people. King David wrote an entire psalm about God's protection and provision for his sheep (Ps 23). In Ezek 34, God's leaders were compared to shepherds, but instead of protecting the sheep, they exploited them and even ate them.

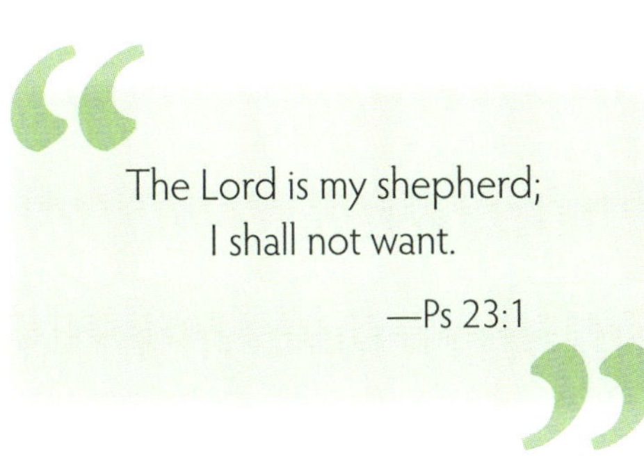

The Lord is my shepherd;
I shall not want.

—Ps 23:1

In John 10, Jesus used an allegory about the shepherd and his sheep to speak about himself, the blind man and the Pharisees.

- Jesus is the shepherd.
- The formerly blind man is represented by the sheep.
- The Pharisees are the predators and thieves.

Jesus said to the Pharisees, "I am the door of the sheep." Just as the sheepfold has only one entrance, the kingdom of God may only be accessed through him (cf. John 14:6). Wonderful blessings await those who find access to God through this door.

> "I am the door. If anyone enters by me, he will be saved and will go in and out and find pasture. The thief comes only to steal and kill and destroy. I came that they may have life and have it abundantly" (John 10:9–10).

> We are his people, and the sheep of his pasture.
>
> —Ps 100:3

He then said, "I am the good shepherd." A shepherd's job was to provide nourishment and water for the sheep. He was also expected to risk life and limb to protect them. How far is Jesus willing to go? All the way, he says. He will die for them.

> "I am the good shepherd. The good shepherd lays down his life for the sheep. . . . I lay down my life for the sheep. . . . For this reason the Father loves me, because I lay down my life that I may take it up again. No one takes it from me, but I lay it down of my own accord. I have authority to lay it down, and I have authority to take it up again. This charge I have received from my Father" (John 10:11, 15, 17–18).

Jesus briefly spoke of "other sheep that are not of this fold" (v. 16). His atoning death was not just for the Jewish nation, but for all nations. Upon the arrival of the church in Acts 2, everyone would be able to enjoy the abundant life promised by the good shepherd, Jesus. We are one flock led by one shepherd (cf. Gal 3:28).

How secure is this sheepfold? According to Jesus, "no one will snatch them out of my hand" and "no one is able to snatch them out of the Father's hand" (John 10:28–29, #111). Because Jesus is the good shepherd, we are protected, as long as we stay in the fold.

Further Division Over Jesus (#101b)

John 10:19–21

Once again, the people were divided in their opinions about Jesus. On the one hand, he had just made lofty claims about himself, compelling those who rejected Jesus to suppose that he must be mad. Some feared he might be demon-possessed. But other people hearkened back to the healing of the blind man. How could someone open the eyes of the blind, they reasoned, and God not have sent him?*

Jesus Again Narrowly Escapes Being Stoned (#111)

John 10:22–39

During the festival, Jesus was walking the temple grounds when he was approached by the religious leaders. They aggressively demanded that he tell them if he was the Christ. Instead of answering their question outright, he suggested that his miracles have already proven his claims (cf. John 3:2, #32b).

Jesus explained further how they weren't listening to him. "My sheep hear my voice," he said, referring to his Good Shepherd discourse from earlier. As the Messiah, Jesus was sent by God the Father to be their good shepherd. And so, as long as they continued to reject Jesus, they were turning their backs on God.

And then, Jesus said something that angered them tremendously: "I and the Father are one." Jesus is one with the Father because he is fulfilling his God-given mission to gather his sheep and lead them, but is also claiming to be on an equal level with God. The Pharisees considered this blasphemous coming from the lips of a mere mortal and intend to stone him to death.

Jesus tries to reason with them by appealing to Ps 82:6. In this passage, human judges were figuratively called "gods" because they represented God in legal matters of the people. As the Messiah sent from God, Jesus could claim this title. "Tell us plainly if you are the Christ," they had demanded. And now, they have their answer. Infuriated with him, the religious leaders attempted to seize Jesus. But, as before, he escaped from their grasp (cf. #99b).

> I said, "You are gods, sons of the Most High, all of you."
>
> —Ps 82:6

* This reference to the healing of the blind man clearly connects the shepherd discourse of John 10:1–18 with the events of John 9. They all go together, despite the awkward chapter division between John 9–10.

Conclusion

As much as he loved the city of Jerusalem and its environs, Jesus knew he had to leave. At this moment, tensions were simply too high, and it was not the time for him to die. He knew his time would be during the Passover in a few months. And so, he and his disciples left Judea.

In the meantime, people in Jerusalem continued to be thinking about him. Right now, many were wondering if he really was the Messiah. Likely, some people were hoping he will declare himself king and lead a revolt against the Roman empire.

Even though he was the rightful king and the Messiah, he had no intention of establishing an earthly kingdom. Instead, he wanted to provide the abundant life—the eternal life—that he promised his sheep. But in order to give them this life, he would have to sacrifice his own life on the cross.

In a few months during Passover, he would do exactly that. Until then, there was still more teaching about the kingdom of God to be done in Perea.

WHAT DID YOU LEARN IN LESSON 10?

Match the key concept in the numbered list below with the letter of the phrase that best describes it. Answers appear upside-down at the bottom of the page.

Key Concepts

1. Hypocrisy
2. Feast of Tabernacles
3. Chorazin
4. Menorah
5. Hanukkah
6. Siloam
7. The Seventy
8. Martha
9. Good Samaritan
10. Central Section
11. Stoning
12. Father of lies

Descriptions

A. A phrase Jesus applied to Satan (John 8:44), while arguing with the religious leaders.

B. The unexpected hero of a parable Jesus told to a lawyer about being a neighbor to others.

C. What Jesus often accused the Pharisees of because they said one thing and practiced another.

D. A major part of Luke's Gospel (Luke 9:51–19:44) during which Jesus travels toward Jerusalem for the last time.

E. One of three cities Jesus condemned because its citizens refused to believe in him after he performed many miracles. This city was north of Capernaum along the Sea of Galilee.

F. An annual week-long holiday that commemorated the 40-year wilderness wanderings of ancient Israel.

G. A candlestick with seven branches used in the temple in Jerusalem. During Hanukkah, the candlestick has nine branches.

H. The woman who complained to Jesus because her sister would not help her prepare the evening meal.

I. The punishment prescribed in the Law of Moses for adultery (Lev 20:10) and blasphemy (Lev 24:16).

J. The group of missionaries Jesus sent to Judea which included the 12 apostles.

K. The location of a pool where Jesus healed the blind man in John 9. The word literally means "sent."

L. An eight-day celebration of the Maccabean revolt. It was first observed in 165 B.C.

Answers

1C, 2F, 3E, 4G, 5L, 6K, 7J, 8H, 9B, 10D, 11I, 12A

WHAT DID YOU LEARN IN LESSON 10?

Do your best to answer the following questions. Some answers can be found in the text of Lesson 10, but not all of them. For others, you will be asked to look up passages in your Bible to find them.

Fill in the Blanks.

1. Near the end of the Feast of Tabernacles, Jesus said, "I am the ______________ of the ______________" (John 8:12, #98).

2. Jesus told the Jews, "You are of your ______________ the ______________" (John 8:44).

3. Jesus told the 70 disciples to rejoice because "your ________ are written in ______________" (Luke 10:20).

4. Which of Lazarus's sisters listened to Jesus instead of serving? ______________

   Which one complained to Jesus because the other wasn't helping to serve? ______________

5. When Jesus' disciples asked him to teach them to pray, what had Jesus been doing (Luke 11:1)? ______________

6. What did the Jews attempt to do after he told them, "I and the Father are one"? ______________

   ____

7. "No, I tell you you, but unless you ______________, you will all likewise ______________" (Luke 13:3).

8. Who did the disciples think was responsible for the blind man's blindness? ______________

   ____

Multiple Choice. Circle the correct answer.

1. What did Jesus do when the woman caught in adultery was brought to him by the scribes and Pharisees?
   A. He condemned her to be stoned to death.
   B. He forgave her and told her not to sin any longer.
   C. He read to her from the Bible.
   D. He embarrassed her by berating her in front of everyone.

2. On two separate occasions, Jews in Jerusalem attempted to stone Jesus to death (John 8:59, #99b; 10:31, #111). Why?
   A. Because they didn't approve of what Jesus was wearing.
   B. Because Jesus healed someone they didn't like.
   C. Because Jesus claimed to be equal with God.
   D. Because they mistook Jesus for a murderer.

3. How did Jesus heal the blind man?
   A. He touched the man's eyes.
   B. He said to him, "Be healed of your blindness."
   C. He made mud by spitting on the ground, anointed his eyes with it and then had him wash it off.
   D. He let one of his disciples heal the man instead.

4. What had the religious leaders threatened to do if anyone confessed Jesus to be the Christ?
   A. He would be stoned to death.
   B. He would be required to pay a fine to the temple.
   C. He was to be congratulated.
   D. He was to be put out of the synagogue.

5. After they witnessed the healing of the blind man, what did people say about Jesus?
   A. He must be mad because of all his lofty claims.
   B. He might be demon-possessed.
   C. He must be sent from God.
   D. All the above.

APPLICATION OF LESSON 10.

For Discussion.

1. Who raised Jesus from the dead? According to passages like Mark 8:31; Luke 24:7; Acts 10:41; 17:3; 1 Thess 4:14 and John 10:17-18, Jesus raised himself from the dead. But normally, the NT speaks of God raising him. ____________________

2. When the Jews heard Jesus say, "Before Abraham was, I am" (John 8:58, #99b), they took up stones, intending to stone him to death. Explain how this statement is a claim by Jesus to be equal with God. ____________________

3. What do you think Jesus means when he says, "I have other sheep that are not of this fold" (John 10:16; cf. Eph 2:13–18)?

LESSON 11

Perean Ministry (#112–127)

Matthew 19–20
Mark 10
Luke 13:22–19:28
John 10:40–11:54

Now more than ever, the religious leaders wanted Jesus dead. Despite their best efforts, he just eluded their grasp yet a second time (John 10:31; cf. John 8:59). But, Jesus knew they would kill him during the Passover in mid-April. Until then, the religious leaders would have to wait because Jesus' "hour had not yet come" (John 8:20).

It was January as Jesus began his Perean Ministry. In a little over three months, he would head back to Jerusalem one final time. For now, he and his apostles left the confines of Palestine and headed northeast into "Judea beyond the Jordan" (Matt 19:1, #122; see Map 11 on page 227). This area, occupied by Jews, was known as Perea. It still wasn't safe here, but the religious leaders were unable to kill him.

From Jerusalem to Perea (#112)

John 10:40–42

The citizens of Perea had great affection for John the Baptist. He had spent a lot of time there, mesmerizing the crowds with his fiery preaching and baptizing many of them. John told them that Jesus was the long-awaited Messiah. And while the Pereans already believed this, their faith was bolstered when Jesus did something for them that John never could do—he performed a miraculous sign. The Pereans' faith and acceptance of Jesus was in sharp contrast to the religious leaders back in Jerusalem.

Luke's Central Section Continues (#113–117)

Luke 13:22–17:10

As he neared the end of his earthly ministry, Jesus became much harsher in his teachings. If you want to enter the kingdom of God, then there is only one option: You must serve him with your whole heart. Jesus will not accept anyone who fails to put him first in his or her life.

Who Will Enter the Kingdom? (#113a)

Luke 13:22–30

A man came up to Jesus and asked him, "Will those who are saved be few?" But Jesus didn't answer his question. Instead, Jesus turned the question back on him, challenging this Jewish man to examine himself. Jesus illustrated entrance into the kingdom of God by comparing it to a narrow door that takes tremendous effort to squeeze through (cf. Matt 7:13). "Many will seek to enter and will not be able to."

Jesus was telling this man that the Jews who think their Jewish heritage was sufficient to grant them access to God would run the risk of being told, "I do not know where you come from." They would stand outside, begging to be let into the kingdom of God. And then Jesus told him that many Gentiles will be granted entrance in place of them.

> "People will come from east and west, and from north and south, and recline at table in the kingdom of God. And behold, some are last who will be first, and some are first who will be last" (Luke 19:29–30).

These non-Jews from the four corners of the world would sit at the banquet feast of God with such dignitaries as Abraham, Isaac, and Jacob and all the prophets, while the Jewish men and women who weren't truly dedicated to Jesus would be denied entrance, shocked that they were barred from the kingdom. "Some who are last will be first," Jesus warned, "and some are first who will be last" (Luke 13:30; cf. Matt 19:30).

Anticipation of Jesus' Death in Jerusalem (#113b)

Luke 13:31–35

A group of Pharisees came to Jesus and urgently pleaded with him to leave Perea immediately, telling him, "Herod wants to kill you." Herod Antipas was the man who had killed Jesus' forerunner,

John the Baptist. In fact, he had imprisoned John at his Perean palace (Josephus, *Ant.* 18.5.2) located near the Dead Sea.

Because Herod also had jurisdiction over Galilee, the Pharisees were obviously trying to bait Jesus into fleeing back to Judea, where the real threat lay waiting for him. Jesus dismissed the supposed threat from Herod Antipas.

> "Go and tell that fox, 'Behold, I cast out demons and perform cures today and tomorrow, and the third day I finish my course. Nevertheless, I must go on my way today and tomorrow and the day following, for it cannot be that a prophet should perish away from Jerusalem'" (Luke 13:32–33).

With these words, Jesus turned his attention to the true threat: Jerusalem (vv. 34–35). He knew he would go to Jerusalem and die. It broke his heart that God's covenant people would reject him, their true Messiah. This was the first of three laments Jesus made on behalf of Jerusalem (Figure 54).

Three Laments over Jerusalem

Description	Citation	Section
"O Jerusalem, Jerusalem, the city that kills the prophets…"	Luke 13:34–35	#113b
And when he drew near and saw the city, he wept over it, saying, "Would that you, even you, had known on this day the things that make for peace!"	Luke 19:41–44	#128b
"O Jerusalem, Jerusalem, the city that kills the prophets…"	Matt 23:37–39	#137b

Figure 54.

Jesus predicted that the people would sing his praises as he entered the city of Jerusalem. This would be fulfilled in Luke 19:38 when Jesus made his triumphal entry into the city (#128b). But the adulation would be short-lived. Amazingly, even though Jesus knew all of this, he would go to Jerusalem anyway. Jesus was never fooled by their accolades.

The Pharisees Lack the Qualities of a Disciple (#114)

Luke 14:1–24

Jesus went to the home of a Pharisee for a Sabbath meal. He and his guests eyed Jesus, watching his every move. A man who had dropsy approached him. Known today as edema, dropsy is a condition that causes tissues to retain too much fluid and can be fatal.

Because it was the Sabbath, Jesus knew the Pharisees would be upset if he healed this man. They considered even such a gracious act to be a violation of the Sabbath. More than likely, this was a trap the Pharisees staged to see how Jesus would respond to the sick man. Anticipating their negative response, Jesus first asked them a pointed question before the healing. "Is it lawful to heal on the Sabbath?"

MIRACLE 32
Healing the Man with Dropsy

When they didn't answer, he proceeded to heal the man and send him on his way. And then, he shined a spotlight on their hypocrisy about "working" on the Sabbath.

> "Which of you, having a son or an ox that has fallen into a well on a Sabbath day, will not immediately pull him out?" (Luke 14:5; cf. Luke 13:15, #110).

The Pharisees were consumed with religious pride. And so, Jesus told two short parables about the importance of humility. He directed the first one to the guests at the banquet (vv. 7–11) and the second to the Pharisee who hosted it (vv. 12–14). These, along with the healing, pointed out their hypocrisy.

- They lacked compassion for the sick man (vv. 1–6)
- They lacked humility toward others (vv. 7–11)
- They lacked concern for the less fortunate (vv. 12–14)

Jesus was demonstrating what citizens of his kingdom are supposed to look and act like. We are to be compassionate, humble, and genuinely concerned for the welfare of others.

PARABLE 24
The Great Supper

Then, in v. 15, someone exclaimed, "Blessed is everyone who will eat bread in the kingdom of God!" In response, Jesus told the parable of the Great Supper (Luke 14:16–24). The Jews were anticipating that just such a divine feast would inaugurate the coming of God's kingdom.

God had already invited them to the Great Supper by sending Jesus. As the Messiah, Jesus was here to inaugurate the kingdom. By rejecting him, the Pharisees declined the invitation they were so anxiously anticipating. Remarkably, those in the parable who were less fortunate had also been invited to the Great Supper. They represented the people the Pharisees disdained, including the "sinners" and tax collectors who, in their humility, had accepted Jesus as the Messiah.

The Cost of Discipleship (#115)

Luke 14:25–35

Many people flocked to Jesus and followed him. As they did, he turned to the crowds and taught them about the cost of becoming one of his disciples.

> "If anyone comes to me and does not hate his own father and mother and wife and children and brothers and sisters, yes, and even his own life, he cannot be my disciple. Whoever does not bear his own cross and come after me cannot be my disciple" (vv. 26–27).

Jesus was telling them, "I must come first in your life." Nothing was more important than him. As he does often, Jesus used hyperbole to emphasize this point. *"You must hate..."* Earlier, he had said that anyone who loved his or her parents "more than me" would forfeit becoming a disciple (Matt 10:37–38, #70b). His harsh language makes us realize how serious our commitment to him has to be. Are you willing to count the cost?

PARABLE 25
Building a Tower and a King Making War

Jesus used two illustrations to impress this point. In the first, a builder miscalculated how much it will cost to construct a tower. He became a laughingstock in the community when he ran out of money (vv. 28–30). In the next illustration, Jesus suggested that a king who was outnumbered two to one should reconsider his options and probably surrender (vv. 31–33). In other words, we, like the builder and the king, must count the cost of discipleship.

Jesus then complimented his disciples by comparing them to salt, which was an important commodity in the first century (vv. 34–35). But salt could go bad and become worthless, he said. If that happened, the salt would be thrown away (cf. Matt 5:13, #54c).

Luke 15:1–32

Three Parables About Repentance (#116)

The Pharisees were scandalized by Jesus' behavior. They were thoroughly embarrassed that he would freely associate with the riffraff of society, including tax collectors and other "sinners." But these were the very people Jesus embraced. By no means did he approve of their sinful behavior. Rather, he had compassion on them, knowing they were genuinely interested in the kingdom of God.

In response to the negativity of the Pharisees, Jesus told a set of three parables. Together, they form a triptych and were intended to be seen together as they created a picture of God's amazing compassion. All three were about lost items (Figure 55).

Three Parables About the Lost

What Was Lost	Action Taken	Response	Citation
One sheep out of a hundred	The shepherd searched	Called friends and neighbors to celebrate	vv. 3–7
One coin out of ten	The woman lit a lamp and searched her house	Called friends and neighbors to celebrate	vv. 8–10
One son out of two	The father waited and watched	Celebrated by killing the fattened calf	vv. 11–32

Figure 55.

PARABLE 26 (see Sec. 91) The Lost Sheep

PARABLE 27 The Lost Coin

In the first parable, a shepherd searched diligently for a lost sheep. He had 99 other sheep safe and accounted for, but he searched everywhere until he found this one that was lost. In the second parable, a woman searched for a lost coin. Although she has nine other coins, she swept her entire home until she finally located the 10th one. In each of these parables, the one doing the searching—the shepherd and the woman—rejoiced greatly when what had been lost was found.

The tax collectors and sinners were represented by the lost sheep and the lost coin. Each of these parables ended by describing angelic celebration over their repentance. The Pharisees seemingly had no idea that they worshiped such a loving God who would send his Son to search diligently for their lost souls. And when he finds them and they return, there is a great celestial celebration.

PARABLE 28
The Lost Son

The third parable drove home this message of grace and love. Often called the parable of the Prodigal Son, it told of a younger brother who demanded that his father give him his portion of the family inheritance immediately. Remarkably, the father did. A few days later, he watched as his younger son left home. In "a far country," the young man squandered all of his inheritance with "prodigal" (KJV) or wasteful living.

The young man fell on hard times and had to find work to keep himself alive. While feeding pigs, which all Jewish men would have found abhorrent, the lost son "came to himself" and decided to return home. But because he had spent his entire inheritance, the young man believed he had forsaken any right to be treated as a son. He intended to ask his father to "treat [him] as one of your hired servants," reasoning that they at least "have more than enough bread" to enjoy as he "[perishes] here with hunger" (v. 17).

In the meantime, the father in the parable had been watching the road, waiting for his wayward child to return. Ignoring his son's prepared speech about becoming a household slave, the father demanded signs of sonship be given to the prodigal, including a robe, a ring and shoes. All had been forgiven! "My son was dead, and is alive again; he was lost and is found" (v. 24).

Everything seemed beautifully resolved, until the older brother heard his younger brother had returned home. Resentful and bitter about the celebratory dinner, the older brother complained to their father. The plight of the older brother was left unresolved as the parable closed with the father reasoning with his older son.

> " 'Son, you are always with me, and all that is mine is yours. It was fitting to celebrate and be glad, for this your brother was dead, and is alive; he was lost, and is found' " (Luke 15:31–32).

The Pharisees were acting like the resentful older brother. They could not fathom that God was displeased with them, especially when they were comparing themselves to "sinners." In this poignant parable, Jesus tried to show them that they too were just as much in need of God's forgiveness, grace and love. Their refusal to rejoice with the salvation of sinners couldn't stop the celebration.

Luke 16:1–13

A Parable About Wealth (#117a)

Throughout his ministry, Jesus emphasized that his followers must be generous and wise with their money. In the Parable of the Unjust Steward, Jesus seemingly praised the dishonesty of a shrewd businessman who had, like the Prodigal Son in the previous parable, wasted his possessions (Luke 16:1; cf. Luke 15:13).

PARABLE 29
The Unjust Steward

At the start of the parable, "there was a rich man" who fired one of his money managers. At first, the "unjust steward" panicked. But then, he formulated a contingency plan by reaching out to debtors who still needed to pay their bills. Instead of requiring the full amount, the manager allowed the business owners to reduce the amount owed. By doing this, he eliminated his own commission and endeared himself to the rich man's clientele. Even the rich man praised the cleverness of his former employee.

Jesus was by no means praising dishonesty, since he labeled this dishonest steward as "unjust." Rather, Jesus was illustrating the importance of effectively managing our material blessings. Failure to do so will cause us to serve money, rather than spending it for the benefit of others.

> "No servant can serve two masters, for either he will hate the one and love the other, or he will be devoted to the one and despise the other. You cannot serve God and money" (Luke 16:13).

Citizens of the kingdom of God should be characterized by generosity and trust in God.

Luke 16:14–31

Another Parable About Wealth (#117b)

The Pharisees loved their money. When they heard Jesus teach on the importance of sharing wealth with others in the previous parable, they openly ridiculed him. In response, Jesus told them another parable, starting with the very same words (v. 19; cf. v. 1).

PARABLE 30
The Rich Man and Lazarus

> "There was a rich man who was clothed in purple and fine linen and who feasted sumptuously every day. And at his gate was laid a poor man named Lazarus, covered with sores" (Luke 16:19–20).

Both of these parables address the point that God will hold us accountable for how we spend our wealth and treat others. The contrast between the rich man and Lazarus could not be starker: one was rich and lived luxuriously while the other was poor and lived in abject poverty. But when both men died, their fortunes were reversed.

Upon opening his eyes in death, the rich man found himself in Gehenna (hell, KJV). Lazarus, who died first, was "carried by the angels to Abraham's side" (v. 22). The rich man saw that Lazarus now sat permanently at the celestial banquet table. He is not *under* the table, as he had been on earth, but is now in a place of honor.

Lazarus

Greek version of Eleazar.
Means "God has helped."

Jesus had a close friend named Lazarus, whom he raised from the dead in John 11:1–44; #118.

Don't confuse Lazarus in the parable with Jesus' friend.

The main point of this parable was not to address where our souls go when we die. Rather, it was a severe condemnation of the Pharisees who think because they had been blessed financially, God must be pleased with them. Little did they realize they will share in the rich man's fate if they continued to reject Jesus. They will *not* sit at the banquet table with Abraham, unless they repented of their covetousness and pride.

Four Lessons on Discipleship (#117c)

Luke 17:1–10

In two lessons on what it means to be a disciple, Jesus challenges us to radically reconsider how we treat another. On the one hand, we must not sin against anyone or cause someone to sin. On the other hand, we must forgive the one who, when rebuked, responds by truly repenting. We have to do this every single time, just like God would for us.

- Do not sin or cause others to sin (vv. 1–2)
- You must always forgive (vv. 3–4)

In response, the apostles said to Jesus, "Increase our faith!" (v. 5). They knew that living these principles was going to be incredibly difficult. Jesus assured them they could do this, for two reasons.

- Because even a small amount of faith has great power (v. 6)
- Because we can always do what God requires (vv. 7–10)

PARABLE 31
Unprofitable Servants

In these two additional lessons on discipleship, Jesus told his apostles they don't need *more* faith, but they just needed to use what they already had (v. 6; cf. Matt 17:20). He illustrated by telling a short parable about a man who had only one household slave. The slave was required not only to work the farm, but also prepare the master's meals. Despite these harsh demands, the slave was never thanked or shown any special treatment because he was doing what was expected of him.

Jesus never demands anything of us he himself has not done. He will never sin against us, of course, and he is always ready to forgive us. And so, if we want to be his disciples, then we must commit to living according to this higher standard. Anything less is unacceptable.

John 11:1–44

Jesus Raises Lazarus from the Dead (#118)

Jesus' ministry in Perea was interrupted when he received an emergency request from some friends in Judea. Lazarus, who lived in Bethany, was on the verge of death. His sisters, Mary and Martha, wanted Jesus to come immediately to heal him. Their urgent message was brief and poignant: "He whom you love is sick."

Because Bethany was so close to Jerusalem, the apostles objected to the idea of making this unexpected trip back to Judea. After all, part of the reason they had gone to Perea in the first place was because, when they had been in the holy city, the Jews had made an attempt on Jesus' life (John 11:8; cf. 10:22–39, #111). Though they feared the worst, Jesus walked by faith, knowing all would be well.

The messengers had said Lazarus was sick, but Jesus knew he was already dead (v. 14). Jesus intentionally stayed in Perea for two additional days (Figure 56). By the time he and his disciples made it back to Bethany, Lazarus had been in the tomb for four days. Jewish culture believed that, after four days, death was irrevocable.

Apparently, Lazarus and his sisters were wealthy and influential citizens of Bethany and as a result, Lazarus' death had brought many mourners to their home who tried to comfort the family. This was a common practice in first-century Jewish culture.

Jesus Raises Lazarus

Prediction	Citation	Section
1. Mary and Martha send word to Jesus in about Lazarus' sickness.	John 11:1–3	#118a
2. Jesus deliberately remains in Perea for two additional days.	John 11:6	#118b
3. Jesus and his disciples travel to Bethany, where he raises Lazarus	John 11:17-44	#119
4. Eyewitnesses report the event to the Sanhedrin	John 11:46-53	#119
5. Jesus travels secretly to Ephraim with the disciples	John 11:54	#119

Figure 56.

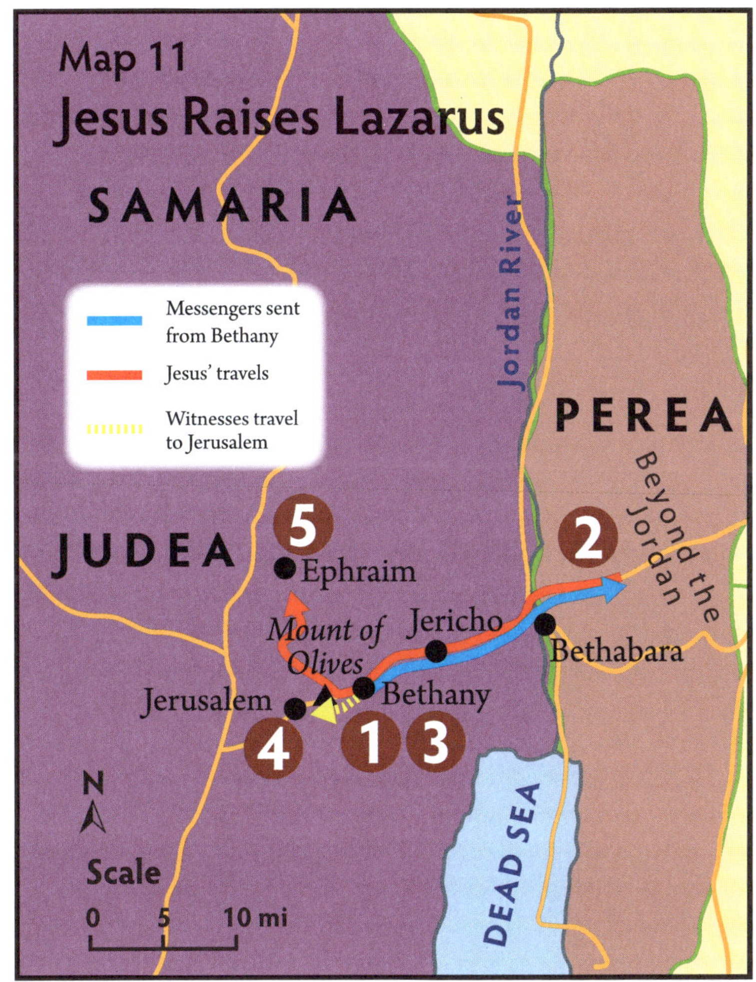

While in the house, Martha and Mary received word that Jesus had finally arrived. Martha made her way to meet him just outside the village. Heartbroken over her brother's death, she could not fathom why Jesus had not hurried to heal Lazarus. "Lord, if you had been here, my brother would not have died" (v. 21).

"Your brother will rise again," Jesus told Martha, to which she responded by saying, "I know that he will rise again in the resurrection on the last day" (v. 24). Jesus then made an incredible claim about himself: "I am the resurrection and the life" (v. 25).

> "I am the resurrection and the life. Whoever believes in me, though he die, yet shall he live, and everyone who lives and believes in me shall never die. Do you believe this?" She said to him, "Yes, Lord; I believe that you are the Christ, the Son of God, who is coming into the world" (John 11:25–27).

Martha's amazing declaration of faith revealed her confidence in Jesus. Even though she didn't understand why he delayed coming to Bethany, Martha placed her hope in Jesus nonetheless.

Martha returned to the house, found Mary and told her, "The Teacher is here and is calling for you" (v. 28). Upon approaching Jesus, Mary fell at his feet, weeping. Through her tears, she spoke the same heart-wrenching words that Martha had: "Lord, if you had been here, my brother would not have died" (v. 32).

Tears welled up in Jesus' eyes, too. He cried with her, deeply moved in his spirit because of her display of sorrow. "Where have you laid him?" he asked. Together, they walked to the tomb. Even though he knew what he was about to do, Jesus was overwhelmed with emotion and wept for the pain his friends were enduring (v. 35). People standing around watching could see how deeply Jesus loved his friends and was distressed at their pain.

> Then Jesus, deeply moved again, came to the tomb. It was a cave, and a stone lay against it. Jesus said, "Take away the stone." Martha, the sister of the dead man, said to him, "Lord, by this time there will be an odor, for he has been dead four days." Jesus said to her, "Did I not tell you that if you believed you would see the glory of God?" (John 11:38–40).

"If you believed, you would see the glory of God." Martha believed Jesus could raise her brother from the dead in the final resurrection. But because Lazarus has been dead for four days, she did not believe it was possible now. Her faith in Jesus was strong, but she was about to truly believe in him.

After composing himself and wording a prayer, Jesus called out: "Lazarus, come out!" To the amazement of everyone, Lazarus walked out of the tomb, wearing his grave cloths. Lazarus is alive!

MIRACLE 33
Raising of Lazarus

The Sanhedrin Plot to Kill Jesus (#119)

John 11:45–54

Many people came to believe that Jesus really was the Messiah after witnessing Jesus raise Lazarus from the dead. Because of Bethany's close proximity to Jerusalem, it did not take long for the Pharisees and the chief priests to learn of these events. And with the Passover only a few weeks away, the religious leaders knew that they had reached the decision to destroy Jesus.

> "If we let [Jesus] go on like this, everyone will believe in him, and the Romans will come and take away both our place and our nation."
>
> —John 11:47–48

Caiaphas was the high priest at this time. He was a Sadducee, part of the Jewish aristocracy and leader of the Jewish ruling body called the Sanhedrin Council. He was closely allied with the Roman governor, Pontius Pilate, who relied on Caiaphas to help him keep the peace in Jerusalem. In large part, it was because of Caiaphas that Jesus would be nailed to the cross in a few weeks.

Teaching on the Way to Jerusalem (#120–127)

Luke 17:11–19:28

At this point in Jesus' ministry, Luke's Central Section (see page 198) coalesces with the Synoptic gospels. The parallel passages in Matthew and Mark clearly indicate that Jesus is finishing his Perean Ministry as he heads to Jerusalem for the last time.

Jesus Heals Ten Lepers (#120a)

Luke 17:11–21

After his visit to Bethany (John 11, #118), Jesus then headed northeast of Jerusalem (cf. John 11:54) and was traveling east and west along the border between Samaria and Galilee. Along the way, he was approached by a group of 10 lepers. They pleaded with Jesus to heal them. He simply said, "Go and show yourselves to the priest," in accordance with the Law of Moses (Lev 13–14). As they went, their leprosy miraculously left them.

MIRACLE 34
Cleansing the Ten Lepers

When they noticed, only one of them stopped and went back to thank Jesus for healing him. a Samaritan. After accepting his gratitude, Jesus then asked, "Where are the nine?"

The healing of the lepers was not just a lesson about gratitude. It revealed the hypocrisy of the Pharisees who saw Jesus perform numerous miracles yet deny he is the Messiah. They were like the nine ungrateful lepers who never returned to glorify God. The Jewish leadership did not accept him, but a Samaritan did.

Since the Pharisees associated miraculous activity with the arrival of the kingdom (cf. Isa 35:6), but denied that Jesus was the Messiah (cf. Matt 12:24, #61; Luke 11:15, #106), they likely asked Jesus about the coming kingdom in mockery. Little did they realize his ministry of healing proved that the kingdom of God was already on its way. In fact, Jesus said, "The kingdom of God *is in your midst*." (Luke 17:21; cf. Luke 11:20, #106). In other words, standing right in front of them was the embodiment of the kingdom.

Luke 17:22–37

The Coming of the Kingdom of God (#120b)

Jesus turned his attention to his disciples and further explained the nature of the kingdom's arrival. Calling it "the day of the Son of Man," he told them no one can predict when it would come. Jesus hinted that the arrival of the kingdom was closely connected to his death.

> "For as the lightning flashes and lights up the sky from one side to the other, so will the Son of Man be in his day. But first he must suffer many things and be rejected by this generation" (Luke 17:24–25).

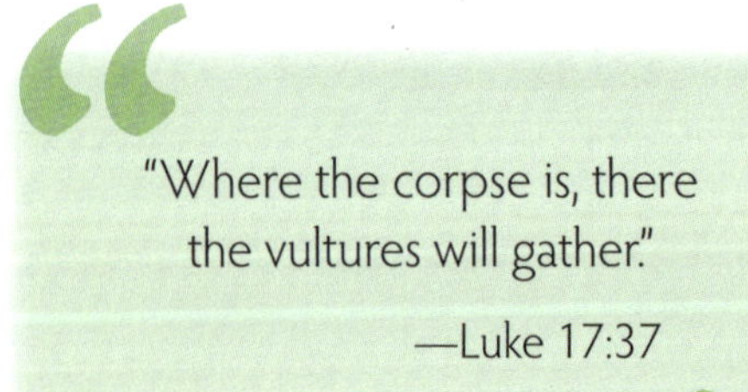
"Where the corpse is, there the vultures will gather."

—Luke 17:37

This proverbial expression denoted judgment. Jesus used it in both Luke 17:37 and Matt 24:28 to describe the destruction of Jerusalem in A.D. 70.

In the Olivet Discourse, Jesus used similar language to describe the destruction of Jerusalem (Matt 24:27, #139e). He even used similar illustrations about the people in the days of Noah who were blissfully unaware of the impending judgment from God (vv. 25–30; cf. Matt 24:37, 139e). The destruction of Jerusalem was, in part, a judgment from God for the Jews' rejection of Jesus. Jesus' death would inaugurate the reign of God in the hearts and lives of humanity. And 40 years later, he would be vindicated when the city that rejected him was destroyed.

Two Parables on Prayer (#121)

Luke 18:1–14

To prepare his disciples for when he was no longer with them, Jesus told two parables about prayer and faithfulness.

The Persistent Widow

PARABLE 32
The Persistent Widow

In the first parable, a godless judge, who lacked compassion for others, was harassed endlessly by a widow. Day after day, she came to the judge, demanding that he give her vengeance against her adversary. The unrighteous judge delivered what she wanted, but only because he wanted her to stop harassing him.

Jesus told this parable so his disciples would never stop praying in the face of persecution. If a godless judge will help someone, then we should know that God, who loves us deeply, will always answer our prayers. And, "he will give justice to [us] speedily." But then, Jesus asked:

> "Nevertheless, when the Son of Man comes, will he find faith on earth?" (Luke 18:8).

The Pharisee and the Tax Collector

PARABLE 33
The Pharisee and the Tax Collector

The second parable answered this question, but in an unexpected way. A Pharisee and a tax collector were both in the temple praying to God. The Pharisee listed all of his great qualities.

> "The Pharisee, standing by himself, prayed thus: 'God, I thank you that I am not like other men, extortioners, unjust, adulterers, or even like this tax collector. I fast twice a week; I give tithes of all that I get'" (Luke 18:11–12).

In sharp contrast to him, the tax collector didn't mention a single accomplishment. Rather, he looked down in humility, praying for mercy and forgiveness, and calling himself the sinner. Jesus then concluded the parable by saying, "This man went down to his house justified, rather than the other."

Because the Pharisees were well respected in Jesus' day, this parable must have shocked everyone who heard it. The Pharisee in the parable was *not* justified, but the despised tax collector was.

When the kingdom of God came, would Jesus "find faith on earth" (Luke 18:8)? Yes, but it wouldn't be found among the religious leaders who were so filled with personal pride they couldn't see the vileness of their own sins and their desperate need for forgiveness. Rather, faith would be in Jesus' disciples who were humble and tenaciously believed in God's love, mercy, and forgiveness.

Marriage and Divorce (#122)

Matt 19:1–12
Mark 10:1–12

While in Perea, Jesus was approached by the Pharisees under false pretenses. Testing him, the Pharisees asked Jesus an emotionally charged question about the right to divorce and remarry. In his response, Jesus appealed to the creation of Adam and Eve.

> "Have you not read that he who created them from the beginning made them male and female, and said, 'Therefore a man shall leave his father and his mother and hold fast to his wife, and the two shall become one flesh'? So they are no longer two but one flesh. What therefore God has joined together, let not man separate" (Matt 19:4–6; see Gen 2:24).

When he told them to obey whatever Moses commanded, the Pharisees quoted from Deut 24:1–4. In this passage, Moses regulated divorce because the rights of women were being disregarded in a male-dominated society.

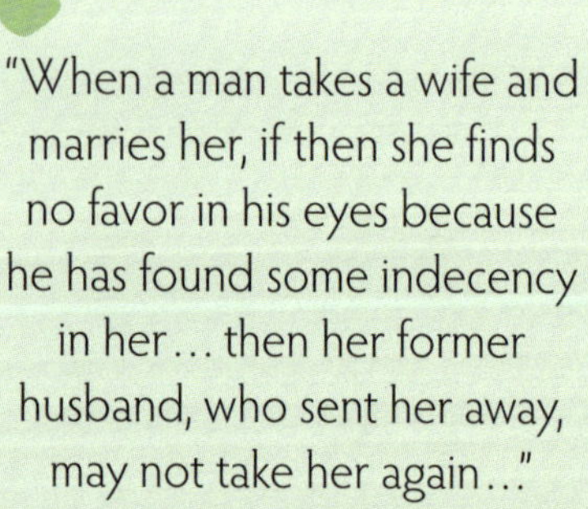

In the first-century world, people were familiar with two schools of thought on this passage. One rabbi, Shammai, said Deut 24:1 refers to sexual immorality only. Another rabbi, Hillel, was much more liberal and interpreted this passage to mean a husband could divorce his wife over anything he deemed indecent. Jesus said that Moses' regulations of divorce were not indications of God's tacit approval of the sinful practice.

> "Whoever divorces his wife, except for sexual immorality, and marries another, commits adultery" (Matt 19:9).

Jesus was emphasizing the importance of people staying married to each other and being faithful to their wedding vows.

Little Children and the Kingdom of God (#123)

Matt 19:13–15
Mark 10:13–16
Luke 18:15–17

Mothers came to Jesus with their children. They wanted him to lay his hands on them and pray. When his disciples tried to prevent them, Jesus insisted they stop. "To such belongs the kingdom of God," Jesus explained, as he embraced the children. Like he had earlier in Capernaum (#90), Jesus once again used children as an example of the child-like humility and innocence that all disciples should possess.

Riches and the Kingdom (#124a)

Matt 19:16–30
Mark 10:17–31
Luke 18:18–30

A young man anxiously approached Jesus. No single Synoptic Gospel identifies him as the rich, young ruler, but these qualities are mentioned. Addressing Jesus as "good teacher, the rich young ruler asked, "What good deed must I do to have eternal life?" Jesus told him to obey the commandments. "Which ones?" he asked. Jesus then proceeded to quote the commandments of Moses that focused on one's relationship with others.

> "You shall not murder, You shall not commit adultery, You shall not steal, You shall not bear false witness, Honor your father and mother, and, You shall love your neighbor as yourself" (Matt 19:18–19; cf. Ex 20:12–16; Lev 19:18).

The last commandment Jesus listed wasn't part of the official Ten Commandments. Rather, it was from Lev 19:18 and embodied the sentiment of the commandments that focused on people's relationships with each other.* (See Parable 42, Matt 25:31–46, #139f.)

The young man genuinely believed that he had kept all of them. And so, he excitedly asked, "What do I lack?" It should come as no surprise that Jesus' answer focused on the rich ruler's love for possessions and his lack of love for others.

> "If you would be perfect, go, sell what you possess and give to the poor, and you will have treasure in heaven; and come, follow me" (Matt 19:21).

This was not the answer the young man wanted to hear. He walked away from Jesus deflated and disappointed.

* Soon, while in Jerusalem, Jesus would refer to this as the second greatest commandment (Mark 12:31, #135; cf. Luke 10:27, #103).

> Jesus, seeing that he had become sad, said, "How difficult it is for those who have wealth to enter the kingdom of God! For it is easier for a camel to go through the eye of a needle than for a rich person to enter the kingdom of God" (Luke 18:24–25).

His disciples were shocked. People in that culture typically thought that anyone who was rich must be exceptionally pleasing to God. Jesus explained that salvation is only possible with God's help. Many who don't think they stand much of a chance are the very people he is seeking.

Jesus then told the 12 apostles they were going to sit on 12 thrones in his kingdom. Obviously, this was not meant to be taken literally, since Judas, his betrayer, was one of the men being addressed. Besides, the kingdom of God is "not of this world" (John 18:36). Rather, Jesus was assuring the apostles that their work in the kingdom was important. Even though they weren't rich, they were extremely valuable to the spreading of the gospel.

Matt 20:1–16

Parable of the Laborers in the Vineyard (#124b)

PARABLE 34
The Laborers in the Vineyard

Only Matthew's account records the parable of the Laborers in the Vineyard, which starts in verse 1 of Matt 20. This parable directly relates to Jesus' message about the rich young ruler and how God is the source of salvation (#124a). It beautifully demonstrates we are all saved by God's grace.

A foreman hired people at different times of the day, promising he would pay all of them a denarius, which was equal to a day's wage (Figure 57). At the end of the workday, those who were hired early in the morning were paid last. They watched as all those who had started after them were paid a denarius. Even those who had only worked for one hour received a full day's wage.

Naturally, those who had worked the entire 12-hour workday anticipated they would receive something extra. They were disappointed when the foreman paid them a denarius like everyone else. But the original agreement had been a day's wage for a day's work. These men who worked 12 hours became resentful of the foreman's generosity toward those who had worked fewer hours.

The Hiring Time of the Laborers

Time of Hiring	Length of Workday	Citation	Amount Paid
Early in the Morning	12 hours	Matt 20:1–2	Denarius
3rd Hour (9 A.M.)	9 hours	Matt 20:3–4	Denarius
6th Hour (noon)	6 hours	Matt 20:5	Denarius
9th Hour (3 P.M.)	3 hours	Matt 20:5	Denarius
11th Hour (5 P.M.)	1 hour	Matt 20:6–7	Denarius

Figure 57.

Having concluded the parable, Jesus then said, "The last will be first, and the first last." Notice the connection between Matt 19:30 and Matt 20:16.

> "Many who are first will be last, and the last first" (Matt 19:30).
>
> "So the last will be first, and the first last" (Matt 20:16).

The Jews believed they were entitled to God's blessings because they as a nation had been God's covenant people since the days of Abraham. But the time was coming when the Gentiles would become equal citizens of the kingdom. We're all saved by God's grace, just the same, and will receive the ultimate reward.

Jesus' Third Direct Prediction of His Death (#125a)

Matt 20:17–19
Mark 10:32–34
Luke 18:31–34

All three Synoptic Gospels record Jesus taking his apostles aside three separate times and explaining to them how he was going die in Jerusalem (Figure 58). This time, though, he was far more descriptive of what would happen to him than the previous two. Jesus plainly told the Twelve he would be condemned to death, mocked, beaten, and crucified, but raised to life after three days.

Jesus' Three Predictions of His Death

Matthew	Mark	Luke	Section
1. Matt 16:21–26	Mark 8:31–37	Luke 9:22–25	#83
2. Matt 17:22–23	Mark 9:30–32	Luke 9:43b–45	#88
3. Matt 20:17–19	Mark 10:32–34	Luke 18:31–34	#125a

Figure 58.

Matt 20:20–28
Mark 10:35–45

Warning Against Ambitious Pride (#125b)

Sensing from these sobering words that Jesus' ministry was nearing its climax, two of Jesus' apostles, James and John, boldly asked Jesus for places of prominence in his coming kingdom. These "sons of thunder" (Mark 3:17) even involved their mother in the request. Jesus could not have been more disappointed with them. They obviously misunderstood completely the spiritual nature of the kingdom of God.

Likely, James and John were motivated by what Jesus had said earlier about the apostles ruling on 12 thrones (#124a). Jesus makes the most of this unfortunate display of raw aspiration and tried yet again to help the apostles see that, in his kingdom, leadership was the opposite of what they thought.

> "Whoever would be great among you must be your servant, and whoever would be first among you must be your slave, even as the Son of Man came not to be served but to serve, and to give his life as a ransom for many" (Matt 20:26–27).

No one exemplifies this attitude of servant leadership better than Jesus, the King of kings and Lord of lords. He left his throne of glory at the right hand of God to come to earth and die on the cross for humanity (2 Cor 8:9). By his life of service for others, Jesus taught us that citizens of his kingdom also must exemplify attitudes of humility, compassion, and love (Phil 2:1–8).

> "Clothe yourselves, all of you, with humility toward one another."
>
> —1 Pet 5:5

Would his apostles ever understand?

Eventually, they would. It is apparent from the writings of Peter and John that, at some point, they grew in their understanding and internalized these lessons from Jesus on how to be a kingdom servant (cf. 1 Pet 5:5; 1 John 4:11).

Matt 20:29–34
Mark 10:46–52
Luke 18:35–43

Healing of Blind Bartimaeus (#126)

A 17-mile road stretched across the Judean countryside, connecting Jericho with Jerusalem. This route had been used for centuries and had been strengthened by the Roman road system of the first century. But before Jesus reached his destination, he performed one last miracle: Jesus healed blind Bartimaeus.

As Jesus first entered the city of Jericho, he and his apostles saw two blind men. One of them was Bartimaeus.* Later, as Jesus was leaving the city, the two men called out for Jesus. Several people told them to quit, but the two blind men called out louder and more desperately. What they said caught Jesus' attention.

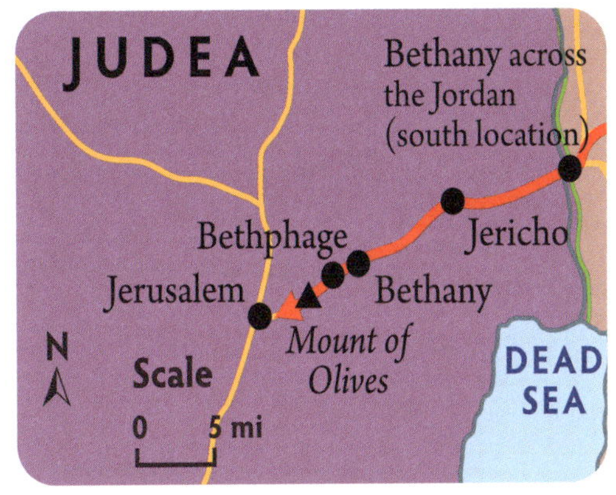

"Lord, have mercy on us, son of David!"

The two blind men saw what others seemingly couldn't. By calling Jesus the son of David, they acknowledged Jesus as the long-awaited Messiah.

Their expression of faith granted them their chance. Bartimaeus and his companion leapt excitedly and made their way to Jesus. Jesus touched their eyes and restored their sight immediately. As Jesus healed them, he said, "Your faith has made you well."

MIRACLE 35 (see Sec. 68)
Healing Two Blind Men

Salvation of Zacchaeus (#127a)

Luke 19:1–10

As Jesus made his way toward Jerusalem, many people had been reaching out to him, including children (Luke 18:15–17, #123), a rich synagogue leader (Luke 18:18–23, #124a), and a blind man (Luke 18:35–43, #126). Zacchaeus was yet another person determined to catch a glimpse of this itinerant preacher.

Among the crowd awaiting Jesus in this Jericho village were many well-respected citizens, but Zacchaeus was not considered to be a member in good standing of his community. As a tax collector, Zacchaeus was despised by the people. He made his living collecting taxes for the Roman empire, which everyone hated. Over the years, as a chief tax collector, Zacchaeus had grown rich off the taxes of the people.

In addition to being greatly disliked, Zacchaeus had another problem. He was incredibly short and would not be able to see over the crowds. He decided to climb a sycamore tree along the path. As the crowds thronged around Jesus, Zacchaeus hoped to catch sight of him from within the tree.

A sycamore tree in the modern-day city of Jericho.

* Matthew states that there were two men, while Mark and Luke only mention Bartimaeus, who was certainly the more prominent of the two.

As Jesus neared the tree along the road, he did something unexpected. He stopped the procession, looked up into the sycamore tree and called Zacchaeus by name. Jesus then said to him, "Come down, for today I must stay at your house" (Luke 19:5).

Zacchaeus was excited. He hurriedly made his way down the tree. No doubt, as was the custom of the day, he and Jesus would have embraced and exchanged kisses on the cheek (just as still is the custom in the Middle East).

As the crowd watched them walk toward Zacchaeus' home, many started complaining. *Doesn't Jesus understand that he has just insulted the elders of the village? How can he not know Zacchaeus is a sinner?*

But Jesus did know the chief tax collector was a sinner. And he also knew Zacchaeus wanted more than simply to "see" Jesus. Zacchaeus also wanted forgiveness and salvation.

> And Zacchaeus stood and said to the Lord, "Behold, Lord, the half of my goods I give to the poor" (Luke 19:8).

While standing with Jesus in front of everyone, this tax collector offered to sell his possessions and to give the proceeds to the poor. This was in sharp contrast to another "rich man" found in Luke 18:18–23 (Figure 59).

Contrast in Character Between the Rich Young Ruler and Zacchaeus

Rich Young Ruler		Zacchaeus	
Rich (and young)	Luke 18:23	Rich	Luke 19:2
Ruler of a synagogue	Luke 18:18	Chief tax collector	Luke 19:2
Well respected in the community	Luke 18:20–21	Disdained by the community	Luke 19:7
Wanted to see Jesus	cf. Mark 10:17	Wanted to see Jesus	Luke 19:3
Refused to sell his possessions and give to the poor	Luke 18:22–23	Volunteered to sell half his possessions and give to the poor	Luke 19:8

Figure 59.

As the ruler of the synagogue, the rich, young ruler was undoubtedly well respected in the community while Zacchaeus as a rich tax collector was disdained by the community. Both rich men had different responses to Jesus. The ruler went away sorrowful at Jesus' admonition to sell his possessions and give to the poor. But Zacchaeus volunteered to sell his possession for the poor.

Zacchaeus made an additional promise: "And if I have defrauded anyone of anything, I restore it fourfold" (Luke 19:8). Not only had Zacchaeus planned to give away large portions of his wealth, but also offered to make restitution to anyone he might have defrauded (cf. Lev 6:5). Jesus responded with beautiful words of forgiveness.

> "Today salvation has come to this house, since he also is a son of Abraham. For the Son of Man came to seek and to save the lost" (Luke 19:9–10).

Parable of the Minas (#127b)

Luke 19:11–28

PARABLE 35 (see Sec. 139f)
The Minas

As people were anticipating the arrival of the kingdom of God, Jesus knew his death would discourage and confuse them. He told a parable to prepare them for its delay. In it, a king left to receive a kingdom (as will Jesus). Before departing, the king entrusted several managers with money, intending for them to invest it.*

Mina
A unit of measurement equal to 100 denarii. (A denarius was a day's wage.)

The king gave each manager a mina. Upon his return, the king was pleasantly pleased that two of the investors had profited tremendously. One of them now had 10 minas and another had five. The king rewarded them with even greater responsibilities.

There was one investor, however, who did nothing with his entrusted mina. Instead of taking responsibility for his failure, this investor blamed the king, saying his standards and expectations were too high. In response, the king took the man's mina and gave it to the one who had 10.

Like those in the parable, there will be those who reject Jesus and those who will squander their opportunity with him. But those who love him and accept him are encouraged to be diligent and patient until the arrival of the kingdom of God.

---

* Be sure to compare Parable 35 with Parable 43 on page 79.

Conclusion

When he raised his friend, Lazarus, from the dead, Jesus proved his words to Martha: "I am the resurrection and the life." Lazarus' death, burial, and resurrection anticipated Jesus' impending victory over death.

But the forces of darkness were closing in on Jesus. The devil and his minions did everything they could to prevent Jesus from accomplishing his ultimate task of saving humanity by murdering him. Unbeknownst to them, however, their efforts to kill Jesus were the very means by which God would conquer sin and death.

As Jesus finished his earthly ministry, he made his way toward Jerusalem. Knowing his death on the cross would happen in the holy city, Jesus continued along the Jericho road toward Jerusalem anyway.

The crucifixion would be brutal and excruciating, but it was absolutely necessary. Jesus' sacrificial death was the only way God's kingdom would come and the only way the sins of humanity could be forgiven.

WHAT DID YOU LEARN IN LESSON 11?

Match the key concept in the numbered list below with the letter of the phrase that best describes it. Answers appear upside-down at the bottom of the page.

Key Concepts

1. Hillel
2. Lazarus
3. Bartimaeus
4. Zacchaeus
5. Gehenna
6. Denarius
7. Kiss on the cheek
8. Bethany
9. Four
10. Shammai
11. Sycamore
12. Dropsy

Descriptions

A. A village about 2 miles east of Jerusalem where Jesus' friends, Lazarus, Martha, and Mary, lived.

B. A customary greeting in the Middle East.

C. A chief tax collector who lived at Jericho.

D. Brother of Martha and Mary of Bethany. He was raised from the dead by Jesus (John 11, #118).

E. A unit of money equal to a day's wage.

F. A blind man Jesus healed at Jericho.

G. A Jewish rabbi in the first century who taught a husband could divorce his wife for virtually any reason.

H. A word sometimes translated as "hell." It refers to the realm of the dead.

I. A jewish rabbi in the first century who believed a husband could only divorce his wife for sexual immorality.

J. A medical condition known today as edema. Jesus angered the Pharisees by healing a man with this disease on the Sabbath.

K. The number of days Lazarus had been in the tomb when Jesus raised him from the dead.

L. The type of tree a short man climbed up in order to see Jesus passing through Jericho.

Answers

1G, 2D, 3F, 4C, 5H, 6E, 7B, 8A, 9K, 10I, 11L, 12J

WHAT DID YOU LEARN IN LESSON 11?

Do your best to answer the following questions. Some answers can be found in the text of Lesson 11, but not all of them. For others, you will be asked to look up passages in your Bible to find them.

Fill in the Blanks.

1. Jesus said, "Some are ____________ who will be first, and some are _________ will be _________ (Luke 13:30, #113a). Explain what he means by this. ____________________

    ____

    ____

2. What were the three parables of the lost about (Luke 15, #116)?

    1. A lost ____________________ Luke 15:3–7
    2. A lost ____________________ Luke 15:8–10
    3. A lost ____________________ Luke 15:11–32

3. After Lazarus died and Jesus arrived in Bethany, Martha and Mary's first words to Jesus were identical (John 11:21, 32). What were they? ______________________________

    ____

4. Why were people so upset when Jesus praised Zacchaeus (Luke 19:6–7, #127a)? ______________________________

    ____

    ____

Multiple Choice. Circle the correct answer.

1. What did Jesus do when he first heard about Lazarus' sickness?

    A. He rushed to Bethany as quickly as he could.
    B. He purposely waited two additional days.
    C. He started but then stopped halfway.
    D. He refused to go because it was dangerous.

2. Why did Jesus lament over the city of Jerusalem?
   A. The Jewish people, led by the religious leaders, were going to reject him as the Messiah during the Passover in Jerusalem.
   B. Because he knew the city was going to be destroyed in A.D. 70 by the Romans.
   C. Worship at the temple has become corrupt under the leadership of the Sadducean priesthood.
   D. All the above.

3. Jesus used two examples to show what it means to the count the cost and follow him (Luke 14:25–35, #115). What were those two examples?
   A. A merchant and a thief.
   B. A soldier and a baker.
   C. A Pharisee and a Sadducee.
   D. A king and a builder.

4. According to Luke 15:1–2, why did Jesus tell the three parables about the lost?
   A. Someone in the audience had lost his wallet.
   B. The Pharisees and scribes were self-righteous and didn't like that "sinners" wanted to be with Jesus.
   C. He wanted to encourage people to work hard.
   D. He needed to settle a dispute between two brothers.

5. What is the main point of the parable of the Rich Man and Lazarus (Luke 16:14–31, #117b).
   A. To tell us where we go after we die and await the final judgment.
   B. To highlight the importance of helping the poor.
   C. To condemn those who believe that, because they are rich, they must be pleasing to God.
   D. To point out the importance of table scraps.

APPLICATION OF LESSON 11.

For Discussion.

1. Why did Jesus have to die by means of crucifixion? Why couldn't he, for example, have drowned instead? Do you think he could have still been our sacrifice for sins? Explain.

____

____

____

2. If Judas hadn't committed suicide after betraying Jesus, do you believed Jesus would have forgiven him, like he did Peter for denying him? Why or why not? ____________________

____

____

____

3. According to Heb 4:15, Jesus never sinned. As the Son of God, *could* he have sinned? And if he had—even just once—could he still have died for the sins of mankind?

____

____

____

4. Did Jesus' human birth to Mary make him less God than the Father or Holy Spirit? ____________________________

____

____

5. Why did the religious leaders reject Jesus? Shouldn't they have been the very ones to recognize him as the Messiah from the Old Testament Scriptures? __________________

____

____

SAT	SUN	MON	TUE	WED	THU	FRI	SAT	SUN
#128a #141	#128b	#129–130	#131–140	#142	#143–152	#153–167	#168	#169–178

LESSON 12

The Final Week (#128–152)

Matt 21:1–26:46
Mark 11:1–14:42
Luke 19:29–22:46
John 11:55–18:1

The word *passion* elicits strong emotion. Its Latin root, *passio*, means "to suffer." That's why the last week of Jesus' life before his crucifixion is often referred to as the passion week. The final week started with his triumphal entry into Jerusalem riding on a donkey (#128b) and would culminate in his painful and humiliating death on the cross.

Arrival at Bethany (#128a)

John 11:55–12:1, 9–11

During his final week, Jesus stayed in Bethany, which was only two miles east of Jerusalem on the eastern side of the Mount of Olives. Very likely, Jesus stayed in the home of Lazarus and his two sisters as he enjoyed their company and their other friends, too. Every day, Jesus and his apostles would travel the short distance to Jerusalem. They did this until Jesus' arrest late Thursday evening or early Friday morning.

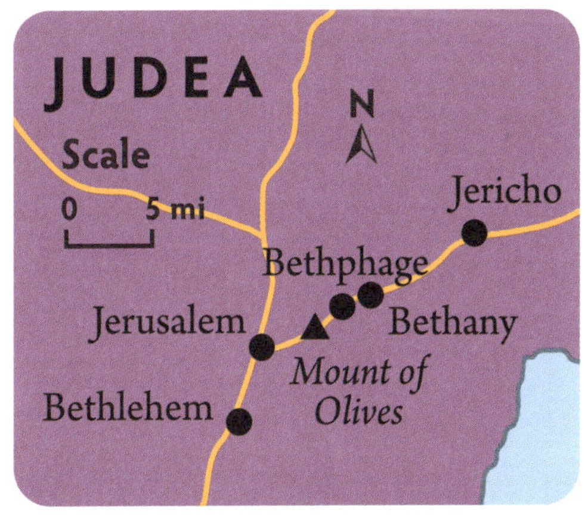

With the Passover only a week away, many people had already made their annual trip to Jerusalem. Because the Law of Moses required the Jews to purify themselves (Num 9:10), many came several days early. The city population was normally 70,000–80,000, but during the Passover and the week-long Feast of Unleavened Bread that immediately followed it, Jerusalem's population would swell to as many as 500,000.

It had been only a few weeks since Jesus had raised Lazarus from the dead at nearby Bethany. In the minds of the majority, this miracle bolstered Jesus' declarations to be the Messiah. They were anticipating he would come to Jerusalem during the feast and announce his claim to David's throne. In fact, many of the people were looking for Jesus, wondering when he would appear.

At the same time, the religious leaders were actively on the lookout for Jesus, too. They wanted to arrest him. They were so desperate to quell this rising movement that they considered murdering Lazarus.

Everybody knew the religious leaders wanted to eliminate Jesus. Anyone with information on where to find Jesus was expected to report it. But, many of the people were quite taken with Jesus. With this mixture of adoration and angst in the city, there was a lot of tension in the city. Like a powder keg, it was ready to explode at any moment.

Mary Anoints Jesus (#141)*

Matt 26:6–13
Mark 14:3–9
John 12:2–8

On the weekend before Jesus' final week, he went to the home of Simon the Leper in Bethany, who hosted a dinner in Jesus' honor. There were quite a few people present, including Lazarus, Martha and Mary, who were Jesus' friends, and his apostles. Many uninvited "guests" also made their way there. They were hoping to see Lazarus, the man who had been raised from the dead, and Jesus, the one who had performed it.

At the dinner, Mary did something quite remarkable. She anointed Jesus with a very expensive ointment called spikenard. This special ointment had to be imported from India, so this was

* While John's Gospel places #141, "Mary Anoints Jesus," on Friday or Saturday of the final week ("six days before the Passover," John 12:1), Matthew and Mark's accounts place Jesus' anointing a few days later, on Tuesday (see Figure 61 on pages 250–251). Likely, John's placement is in the correct chronological order, while Matthew and Mark have rearranged #141 for thematic purposes. In the previous section (#140), the religious leaders are plotting to murder Jesus. Their animosity sharply contrasts with Mary's adoration and worship of him in #141.

something she had planned well in advance. Mary wanted to demonstrate her love and appreciation for Jesus. He had, after all, recently restored Lazarus to her and her sister, Martha.

The ointment was about a pint of pure nard, the plant from which spikenard comes. To preserve the aroma, the ointment was contained in an alabaster jar. Once the container was opened, its wonderful fragrance filled the house. Mary poured the expensive ointment on Jesus' head and feet and used her hair to wipe it.

The dried roots and stems of the nard plant are used to produce an expensive oil called spikenard.

The ointment was valued at "three hundred denarii" by one of the dinner guests (John 12:5). Worth "more than a year's wage," some deemed Mary's action to be too extravagant and a waste of money (Mark 14:5). "The ointment should have been sold," they said, "and the money given to the poor."

One of those indignant dinner guests was Judas Iscariot. As the treasurer for Jesus' band of apostles, Judas would often steal coins from their collective money bag. Despite his words of protestation, he had no concern for the poor, only for himself.

Jesus had a very different reaction. "Leave her alone," he insisted and proceeded to praise Mary for her demonstration of sacrificial love.

> "For you always have the poor with you, and whenever you want, you can do good for them. But you will not always have me. She has done what she could; she has anointed my body beforehand for burial. And truly, I say to you, wherever the gospel is proclaimed in the whole world, what she has done will be told in memory of her" (Mark 14:7–9).

"You will not *always have me."* A sense of forboding must have come over the room when Jesus said this. Jesus had already told the apostles about his crucifixion twice before (see Figure 46 on page 177 of volume 1). Within the week, Jesus would be dead. This was a third prediction of his impending death on the cross.

SUNDAY

Matt 21:1–11, 14–17
Mark 11:1–11
Luke 19:29–44
John 12:12–19

The Triumphal Entry (#128b)

On Sunday of the final week, Jesus and his apostles left Bethany to go to the Mount of Olives. He intended to make his triumphal entry into Jerusalem by descending the mountain and following a path that led into the city.

The triumphal entry marked the beginning of the end. Afterward, there was no turning back. The political waters were permanently stirred now as Jesus staked his claim to David's throne. He did this by deliberately arranging to have a donkey and her young colt brought to him, just as previous kings of Israel had done, too (Figure 60). He then rode this colt into Jerusalem.

Passages Fulfilled in Jesus' Triumphal Entry

Old Testament Passage	Citation	Explanation
Behold, your king is coming to you; righteous and having salvation is he, humble and **mounted on a donkey**, on a colt, the foal of a donkey.	Zech 9:9	This verse is quoted in Matt 21:5
Save us, we pray, O LORD! O LORD, we pray, give us success! Blessed is he who comes in the name of the LORD!	Ps 118:25–26	This passage is quoted in Matt 21:9; Mark 11:9; Luke 19:38; John 12:13
And [David] the king said to them, "…Have Solomon my son ride on my own mule, and bring him down to Gihon [to be anointed king]."	1 Kings 1:33	Just as Solomon had ridden David's mule into the city at his inauguration, Jesus did the same
Then in haste every man of them took his garment and put it under him on the bare steps, and they blew the trumpet and proclaimed, "Jehu is king."	2 Kings 9:13	When Jehu was anointed king of Israel, the people had spread their garments before him

Figure 60.

Hosanna

An abbreviation of "Save, we pray" (Ps 118:25).

Hosanna came to be used as an expression of adoration, praise, or joy.

The implications of his actions were not missed by the people. Someone shouted, "Blessed is the coming kingdom of our father David!" (Mark 11:10). People removed their outer garments and laid them down along a path. Others cut palm branches in celebration of his arrival, using them to also pave the path. Songs of praise were sung to Jesus. "Hosanna!" they cried. "Hosanna to the son of David!"

Not everyone, however, was elated with this royal procession. The Pharisees demanded that Jesus tell the people to cease and desist. But he refused. "If these were silent," he told them, "the very stones would cry out" (Luke 19:39–40). The people were enthralled with this prophet of God who had called Lazarus from the tomb and had just entered Jerusalem in such kingly fashion. Jesus had incurred the anger of the religious leaders. "The world has gone after him!" they lamented (John 12:19).

A donkey with her young colt.

They were convinced Jesus must be stopped. *But how?* They would accomplish this by turning the fickle crowd against Jesus. Today, on Sunday, the people loved him. But by Thursday of this final week, the religious leaders would have persuaded the people that Jesus was not their king, but an imposter.

As he approached Jerusalem, Jesus saw the sprawling city before him and momentarily stopped the procession. Despite the happiness of the moment, his mood suddenly changed. He knew the people would ultimately reject him as their king and instead demand his crucifixion.

That wasn't the main reason he wept for the city. Jesus also knew that in 40 years, in A.D. 70, the city would be completely destroyed by the Roman general, Titus, and that their rejection of him at this moment in time would play a large part in the city's judgment.

> And when he drew near and saw the city, he wept over it, saying, "Would that you, even you, had known on this day the things that make for peace! But now they are hidden from your eyes" (Luke 19:41–42).

He went on to add, "You did not know the time of your visitation" (Luke 19:44), in part, referring to his triumphal entry into Jerusalem. This was the Jews' chance to accept Jesus as their Messiah. However, their preconceived notions prevented them from embracing his vision of Israel's redemption (cf. Luke 24:21). The king had arrived, but he was going to be rejected. Seeing the city at this crucial moment was too much for Jesus to bear, causing him to weep over the city (see Figure 54 on page 29).

After his triumphal entry, Jesus looked around in the temple, but soon afterward returned to Bethany for the night with his apostles (Mark 11:11; see #128b in Figure 61).

THE FINAL WEEK (#128–168)

Sunday		Monday		Tuesday	
Jesus makes his triumphal entry into Jerusalem	#128b	On the way from Bethany to Jerusalem, Jesus curses the fig tree	#129a	In the morning, on the way back to Jerusalem, the disciples see the withered fig tree	#131
Jesus briefly views the temple and returns to Bethany (Mark 11:11)	#128b	Jesus cleanses the temple	#129b	In Jerusalem, the religious leaders question Jesus' authority	#132–138
		The crowds in Jerusalem share their opinions about Jesus (might have occurred on Wednesday, since Jesus hid himself from the crowds afterwards, John 12:36b)	#130	Jesus predicts the destruction of the temple and his return (Olivet Discourse)	#139
				The Sanhedrin plots to arrest and kill Jesus	#140
				In Bethany, Mary anoints Jesus for burial (this probably took place on Saturday, #128b)	#141

Figure 61.

Jesus still had much to teach his apostles, but they would not understand it all until after his crucifixion and resurrection. Then they would know that this final week changed everything forever.

Wednesday		Thursday		Friday	
Judas agrees to betray Jesus	#142	In the Upper Room, Jesus eats the Passover and institutes the Lord's Supper	#143–148	Jesus is arrested in the Garden of Gethsemane	#153
		The Farewell Discourse	#149–151	**Jewish Trial** Phase 1: Annas	#154
		Jesus prays in the Garden of Gethsemane	#152	**Jewish Trial** Phase 2: Caiaphas and a quorum of the Sanhedrin	#155
				Peter's denials	#156
				Jewish Trial Phase 3: Sanhedrin Council	#157
				Judas hangs himself	#158
				Roman Trial Phase 1: Pilate Phase 2: Herod Antipas Phase 3: Pilate again	#159–161
				Jesus is crucified	#162–166
				As the sun sets, Jesus is buried in the tomb of Joseph of Arimathea	#167

Saturday	
The religious leaders secure Jesus' tomb	#168

MONDAY

Matt 21:12–13, 18–22
Mark 11:12–25
Luke 19:37–38, 45–48
John 12:20–50

Lessons From the Fig Tree (#129–131)

On the following morning as Jesus and his apostles were making the return trip back to Jerusalem from Bethany, Jesus stopped at a leafy fig tree—and cursed it! At day's end as they made their way back to Bethany, the apostles saw this beautiful fig tree shriveled up and dead.

Why would Jesus do this?

Matt 21:18–19a
Mark 11:12–14

Jesus Curses the Fig Tree (#129a)

MIRACLE 36
Withering the Fig Tree

Although the tree was covered in leaves, there was no reason to expect any fruit. Fig season was a couple months away, in late June. But Jesus was hungry and, finding no figs, he cursed the tree. "May no fruit ever come from you again!"

The fig tree's demise would serve as a powerful teaching tool for his apostles (see #131 on page 257). When they saw the withered fig tree later that evening, the events of the day flooded their minds, and they realized the cursing of the fig tree was never really about figs, but about the Jewish nation and its rejection of him.

Matt 21:12–13
Mark 11:15–18
Luke 19:45–48

The Second Cleansing of the Temple (#129b)

As Jesus and his apostles made their way to Jerusalem, they arrived at the temple grounds. People were inside the Court of the Gentiles buying animals to sacrifice for Passover. The smell and the noise must have been hard for Jesus to take, especially since the temple always held such a high priority in his life.

Seeing the desecration of the temple by these merchants, Jesus started overturning tables and chairs. He had done this before at the beginning of his ministry.* It was three years ago, at the same time of year, just days before the Passover. On both occasions, there were many animals in the temple court—sheep, cattle, and pigeons—and the exchanging of money taking place. And then, he cleansed the temple again, at the end of his earthly ministry.

* Only John's Gospel records the first cleansing of the temple (John 2:13–22, #31). The Synoptics record the second cleansing at the end of Jesus' ministry (#129b).

In explaining his actions, Jesus quoted from Isa 56:7 and Jer 7:11.

> "Is it not written, 'My house shall be called a house of prayer for all the nations'? But you have made it a den of robbers" (Mark 11:17).

A beautiful fig tree full of leaves.

Notice that Jesus said the temple was to be "a house of prayer for *all the nations*." In Isa 56, God said he wanted people of all nations to enjoy salvation. The temple was to serve as a beacon for all people to make their way to the one true God. Was it too much to ask God's covenant people, the Jews, to provide an example to them? Here, in the Court of the Gentiles, the Jewish merchants were making a mockery of God's house by treating it as a common place for animal trade (cf. John 2:16).

The "den of robbers" was from Jeremiah's scathing temple sermon (Jer 7:1–8:3). Just like the Jews in Jesus' day, God's covenant people in Jeremiah's day had corrupted the temple. In Jer 8:13, the prophet made a statement that fits very well with Jesus' illustration of the fig tree from earlier in the day (see Mark 11:13, #129a).

> "When I would gather them, declares the LORD,
> there are no grapes on the vine,
> *nor figs on the fig tree;*
> even the leaves are withered,
> and what I gave them has passed away from them."

Jesus used the fig tree to illustrate the fact that God is always hungry for his people's hearts. God's people should be bearing fruit always, not just when it's time for an annual festival. Instead, God's people have "robbed" God by depriving him of their heartfelt worship.

"We Wish to See Jesus" (#130a)

John 12:20–36a

A group of Gentiles who had come for the Passover approached Philip the apostle. "Sir, we wish to see Jesus," they told him. Ironically, the Pharisees had recently said "the world has gone after him" (#128, John 12:19). Clearly, they were on to something, whether they realized it or not.

1 The **Gate of the Essenes** allowed the Essenes to access latrines outside the city walls in accordance with their strict laws of hygiene.

2 **Herod's Palace** was the Jerusalem home of Herod the Great from 23 to 4 B.C. Pilate, who normally resided in Caesarea Maritima, resided in this palace during his visits to Jerusalem, including his visit for the Passover preceding Christ's crucifixion.

3 The **Praetorium** was in Herod's Palace (Matt. 27:27; Mark 15:16), which served as Pilate's official headquarters and as a fortress. A raised stone pavement, used for official judgments, stood outside the palace and was the site of Jesus' condemnation under Pilate (John 19:13).

4 5 6 Herod the Great fortified three towers to protect his palace: from west to east there was the **Tower of Hippicus** (155 feet/47 m tall), the **Tower of Phasael** (138 feet/42 m tall), and the **Tower of Mariamne** (95 feet/29 m tall).

7 The two-level **Palatial Mansion** (6,500 sq. feet/604 sq. m) may have been the Palace of Annas, who served as high priest from A.D. 6 to 15. Annas's son-in-law Caiaphas held this office from A.D. 18 to 36 and presided at the trial of Jesus (Matt. 26:57).

8 This is often considered the most likely location of **Golgotha,** the place of Jesus' death. It was on a hill overlooking a quarry, outside the Second Wall of the city and near the Gennath (Garden) Gate.

9 Herod the Great lived in the luxurious **Hasmonean Palace** from the mid-30s to 23 B.C. while awaiting the building of his own new palace. Herod Antipas ("Herod the Tetrarch") lived in this palace during his reign, 4 B.C.–A.D. 39. Jesus appeared before him here in either A.D. 30 or 33.

10 The **Archives** building contained the public registers (including genealogies) as well as bonds taken by moneylenders, which allowed the recovery of debts.

11 The **Xystus,** built on the site of the former Greek Gymnasium, was a place of mass assembly.

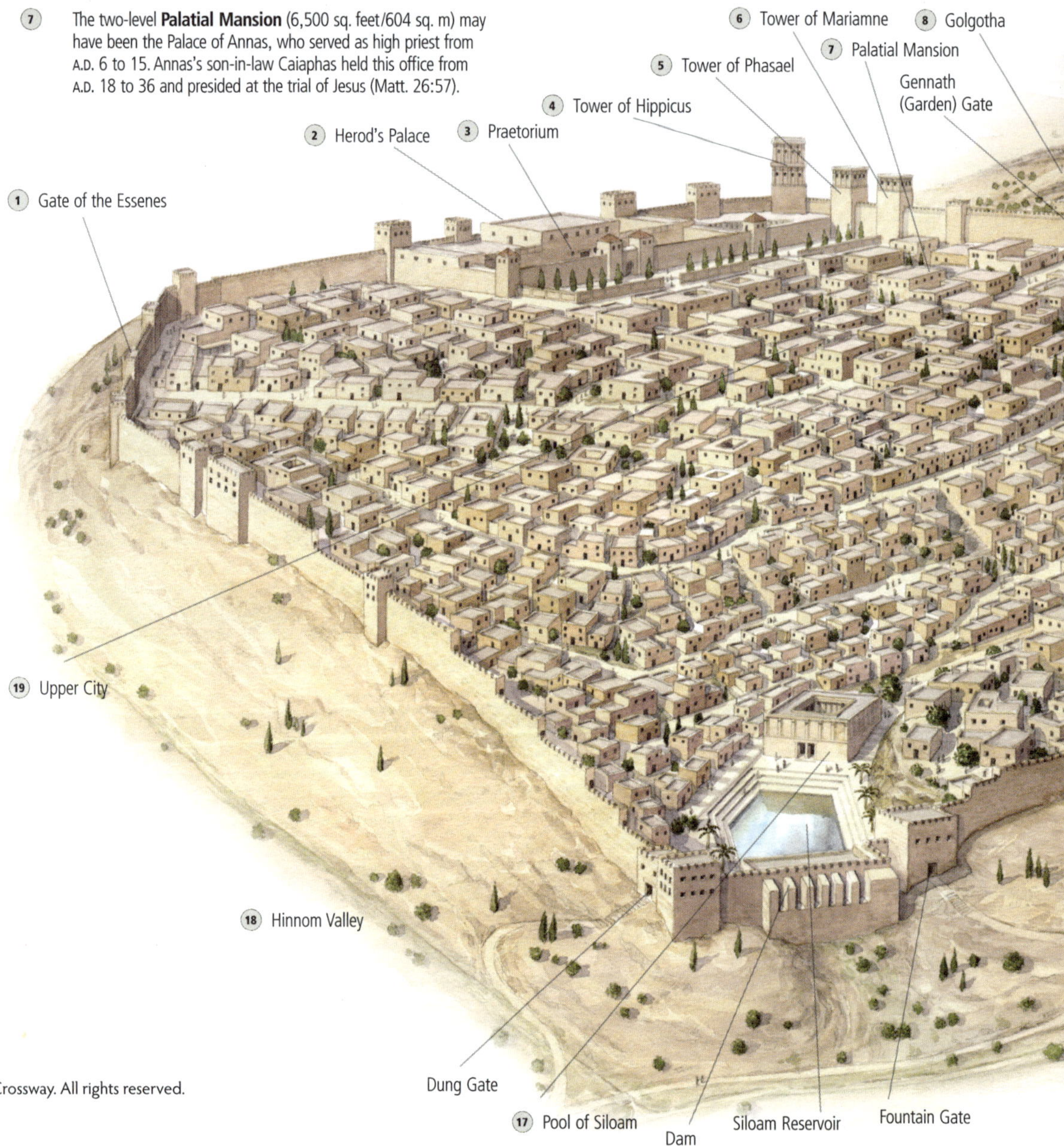

(12) The **Council House** was a public building, perhaps functioning as a municipal office.

(13) **The Temple** was reconstructed by Herod the Great, beginning in 20/19 B.C.

(14) The **Bethesda Pools** (see John 5:2) were twin pools, each measuring c. 312 by 164–196 feet (95 by 50–60 m), and c. 50 feet (15 m) deep. A small Roman temple dedicated to Aesculapius stood to the east of the pools.

(15) The **Garden of Gethsemane** was located approximately 300 yards (274 m) from Jerusalem and the Temple Mount. The Mount of Olives was "a Sabbath day's journey away" from Jerusalem (Acts 1:12), approximately 1,100 yards, or 3/5 of a mile.

(16) The ravine of the **Kidron Valley** has always served as Jerusalem's eastern boundary.

(17) The **Pool of Siloam** (cf. John 9:7), a focal point of Jerusalem, adjoined a large dam and reservoir, and received water from the Gihon Spring.

(18) The **Hinnom Valley** was to the south of the hill that was the original city of David.

(19) The **Upper City** housed luxurious villas of wealthy residents in the Herodian period.

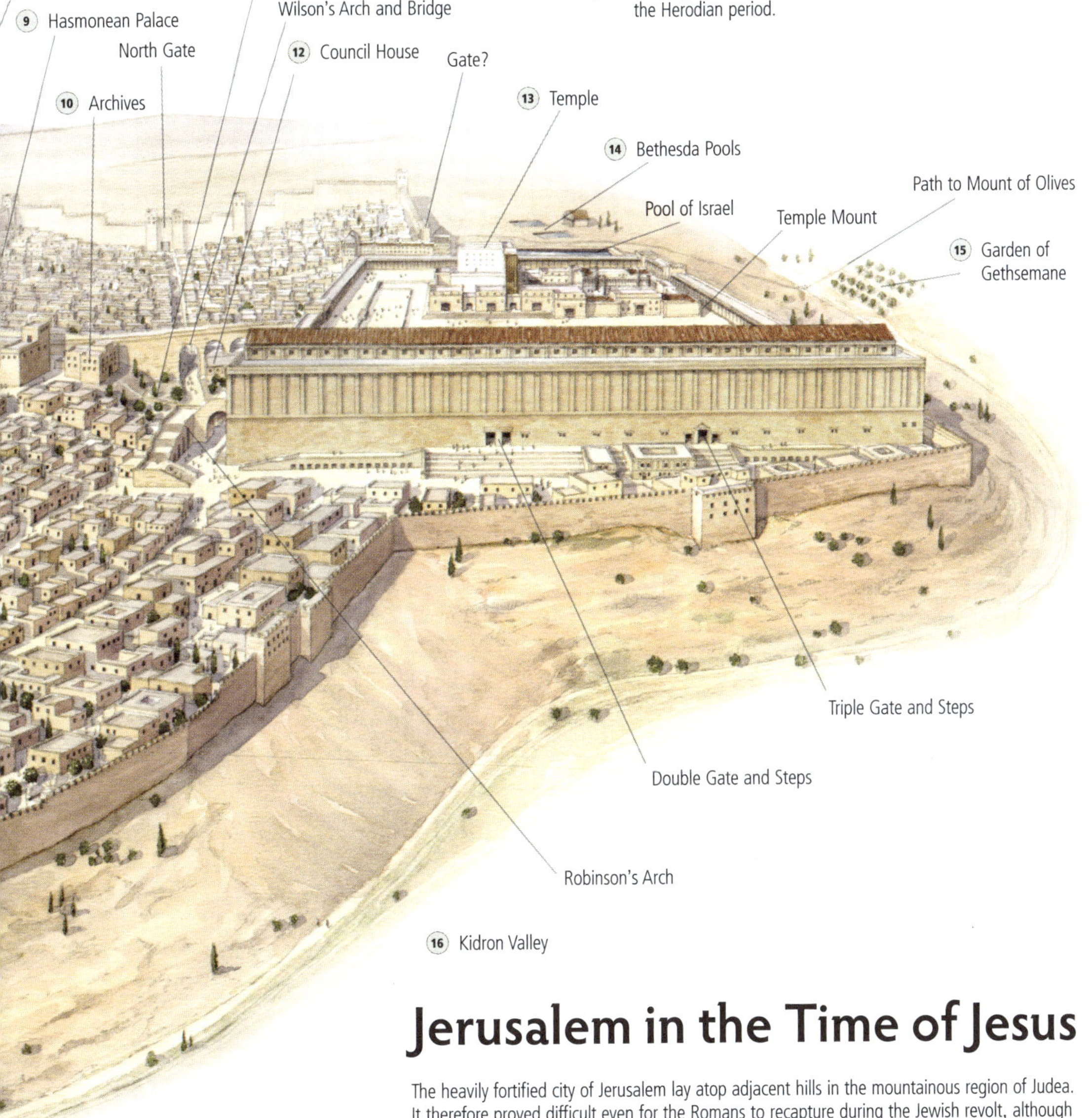

Jerusalem in the Time of Jesus

The heavily fortified city of Jerusalem lay atop adjacent hills in the mountainous region of Judea. It therefore proved difficult even for the Romans to recapture during the Jewish revolt, although they eventually did so in A.D. 70 after a bitter siege. The oldest portion of Jerusalem, called "the city of David" and "Mount Zion," lay to the south of the temple, but the city walls in the first century also encompassed the newer Upper City to the west of the temple. To the east, across the Kidron Valley (John 18:1), stood the Mount of Olives (Mark 13:3). To the south of Zion lay the Hinnom Valley. The reconstruction above depicts Jerusalem around A.D. 30, and the general direction of the drawing is looking north.

Philip found Andrew and together they approach Jesus. Instead of speaking with the Gentiles, he took this moment to teach his apostles yet again about the necessity of his impending death. "The hour has come for the Son of Man to be glorified," he told them (v. 23).

Here, close to the end of his ministry, Jesus must have startled his apostles when he said his hour "has come." He had repeatedly told them his hour had *not* yet come (John 2:4, #29; 8:20, 98). He knew what no one else did: his death on the cross was only days away. The apostles needed to understand Jesus could be glorified only if he died (cf. Luke 24:26, #176).

> "Unless a grain of wheat falls into the earth and dies, it remains alone; but if it dies, it bears much fruit" (John 12:24).

Jesus was talking about himself when he said this. He came to die. In the next few verses, we see the human side of Jesus as he spoke of how difficult his death on the cross would be for him. He knew the crucifixion and the events leading up to it were going to be brutally painful. Would Jesus really go through with it?

> "Now is my soul troubled. And what shall I say? 'Father, save me from this hour'? But for this purpose I have come to this hour. Father, glorify your name." Then a voice came from heaven: "I have glorified it, and I will glorify it again" (John 12:27–28).

The voice of God the Father himself had spoken. The people standing nearby heard the voice, but didn't understand it. Perhaps they thought it was the rumblings of thunder. Others perceived an angel had spoken with him. Both were wrong.

> "Jesus, . . . for the joy that was set before him, endured the cross, despising the shame."
>
> —Heb 12:2

God spoke from heaven in order to strengthen his Son before his encounter with the cross (cf. Luke 3:22, #74). Jesus' was willing to endure the cross, despite how difficult it would be (Heb 12:2).

> "And I, when I am lifted up from the earth, will draw all people to myself." He said this to show by what kind of death he was going to die (John 12:32–33).

His "hour has come" to finish what he started. And finish it, he would (John 19:30).

Different Responses to Jesus (#130b)

John 12:36b–50

All throughout the final week, Jesus taught not just his apostles, but also the crowds (see Luke 19:47–48). He challenged the Twelve and others to accept him as the Messiah, and many did. Despite their conviction in Jesus, Jewish leaders refused to confess their faith, for fear of its repercussions.

> Many even of the authorities believed in him, but for fear of the Pharisees they did not confess it, so that they would not be put out of the synagogue; for they loved the glory that comes from man more than the glory that comes from God (John 12:42–43).

Of course, a great many throughout Jesus' ministry never came to believe in him at all. People who had seen the miracles refused to accept him as the Son of God. And yet, Jesus would gladly die for all of them, too.

"Have Faith in God" (#131)

TUESDAY

Matt 21:19b–22
Mark 11:19–26
Luke 21:37–38

In the morning, as Jesus and his disciples were heading back to Jerusalem, they passed by the fig tree he had cursed the day before (#129a). It was completely withered! Peter shouted, "Rabbi, look! The fig tree that you cursed has withered." Jesus responded by issuing a command.

> "Have faith in God. Truly, I say to you, whoever says to this mountain, 'Be taken up and thrown into the sea,' and does not doubt in his heart, but believes that what he says will come to pass, it will be done for him" (Mark 11:22b–23).

The previous day's cursing of the fig tree and the cleansing of the temple were about the people's lack of faith in God (#129a). On the one hand, there were those who had no confidence in God's power. Like the leafy fig tree, they appeared faithful on the outside, but by their actions, they demonstrated their unfaithfulness. In contrast to them, we must have a genuine love and passion for God, believing that he can move mountains for us.

Jesus also emphasized the importance of forgiveness (Mark 12:24–25). Effective prayer requires faith and forgiveness. While on the cross, Jesus would demonstrate both.

Matt 21:23–22:40
Mark 11:27–12:34
Luke 20:1–40

Challenges to Jesus' Authority (#132–135)

On Tuesday of the final week, Jesus was confronted by the religious leaders with a series of trick questions (Figure 62). They were hoping to entrap Jesus with his answers. Instead, Jesus confounded them with his answers, to the delight of the crowds who were observing (Matt 21:46; Mark 12:12–13; Luke 20:19–20).

People had gathered that morning to hear Jesus teach in the temple (cf. Luke 21:38). They were mesmerized by how brilliantly Jesus handled every trick question thrown at him (cf. Luke 19:48). Even the religious leaders were amazed by Jesus (Matt 22:22; Luke 20:26, 39–40).

Matt 21:23–22:14
Mark 11:27–12:12
Luke 20:1–19

Challenge #1: "By What Authority…?" (#132)

The chief priests, scribes, and elders attacked Jesus first. They asked him, "By what authority are you doing these things?" No doubt, "these things" included yesterday's cleansing of the temple.

Jesus knew they would never be satisfied with anything he said. And so, instead of answering them, he said, "I also will ask you one question." Jesus ingeniously asks them, "The baptism of John, from where did it come? From heaven or from men?" He knew the crowds of people listening respected John the Baptist as a prophet. Therefore, the religious leaders, who didn't believe John was the messenger sent from God, refused to answer. "Neither will I tell you by what authority I do these things," Jesus said.

PARABLE 36
The Two Sons

PARABLE 37
The Wicked Vinedressers

PARABLE 38
The Wedding Feast

But he wasn't finished. Jesus proceeded to tell a series of three parables directed against the religious establishment.

- The Two Sons (Matt 21:28–32)
- The Wicked Vinedressers (Matt 21:33–45; Mark 12:1–12; Luke 20:9–19)
- The Wedding Feast (Matt 22:2–14)

These parables were scathing indictments against them, and they knew it (Matt 21:45). Because the chief priests, scribes and elders did not accept Jesus as the Messiah, they rejected God's will. In the parable of the wicked vinedressers, Jesus identified himself as the cornerstone spoken about in Ps 118:22–23. "When it falls on anyone, it will crush them," he said ominously.

Tuesday's Challengers

Religious Leaders	Question Asked	Section
Chief priests, scribes, and elders	"By what authority are you doing these things?"	#132
Pharisees and Herodians	"Is it lawful to pay taxes to Caesar?"	#133
Sadducees	"In the resurrection, whose will she be?"	#134
Scribe by himself	"What is the greatest commandment?"	#135

Figure 62.

Challenge #2: "Is it Lawful to Pay Taxes?" (#133)

Matt 22:15–22
Mark 12:13–17
Luke 20:20–26

The Pharisees and Herodians, normally at odds with each other, came together to intentionally ask a political question that easily could have gotten Jesus in trouble with the people. Wanting to entangle him in his words (Matt 22:15), they asked, "Is it lawful to pay taxes to Caesar?" They thought there was no way Jesus could tiptoe around this explosive question.

A first-century silver denarius, featuring the image of Tiberias. The Jews were deeply offended by the image of Caesar.

They were wrong. "Who's inscription is on the denarius?" Jesus asked them. When they responded, "Caesar's," Jesus gave his brilliant comeback: "Render to Caesar the things that are Caesar's, and to God the things that are God's." In other words, as long as Rome is in power, the Jewish people should pay their taxes. But by rejecting Jesus, the religious leaders were not rendering to God what was rightfully his—obedience.

Challenge #3: "Who's Wife Will She Be?" (#134)

Matt 22:23–33
Mark 12:18–27
Luke 20:27–40

The Sadducees took their turn at trying to entrap Jesus. Because they did not believe in the reality of the resurrection, they asked an unanswerable question related to it. "If a woman marries seven brothers, in the resurrection, whose wife will she be?" Obviously, they think they are clever. But by asking this ridiculous riddle, they were showing their desperation to rid themselves of Jesus.

Jesus humiliated the Sadducees by saying, "You are wrong, because you know neither the Scriptures nor the power of God." He then proceeded to quote from Ex 3 where God identified himself as the God of Abraham, Isaac, and Jacob. Jesus explained that, even though these men were physically dead, their eternal souls were still alive. God "is not God of the dead, but of the living." These powerful leaders were thoroughly embarrassed.

Matt 22:34–40
Mark 12:28–34

Challenge #4: "The Greatest Commandment?" (#135)

At last, on this busy Tuesday at the temple, Jesus was approached by one final challenger. The Pharisees decided to send a solitary scribe who was an expert in the law of Moses. He asked Jesus, "What is the greatest commandment?" Jesus' answered him:

> "You shall love the Lord your God with all your heart and with all your soul and with all your mind. This is the great and first commandment. And a second is like it: You shall love your neighbor as yourself. On these two commandments depend all the Law and the Prophets" (Matt 22:37–39).

When the scribe responded by adding that obeying these commandments was more than important than any offering, Jesus responded favorably: "You are not far from the kingdom of God." Unlike many of his fellow Pharisees, this man seemed to be well on his way to embracing Jesus' teachings on true righteousness.

Matt 22:41–23:39
Mark 12:35–44
Luke 20:41–21:4

Jesus' Response to the Challenges (#136–138)

By now it was apparent no one was going to entrap Jesus. After Jesus finished answering their questions, he then asked some questions of the religious leaders. Jesus' intention was to teach the people watching and listening.

Matt 22:41–46
Mark 12:35–37
Luke 20:41–44

Response #1: "Who's Son is He?" (#136)

Jesus asked the Pharisees a question about the identity of the Messiah. He quoted Ps 110:1, which identifies the Messiah as both God's son and David's son.

> " 'The Lord [i.e., God] said to my Lord [i.e., David's son],
> "Sit at my right hand,
> until I put your enemies under your feet" ' "? (Matt 22:44).

He asks them, "How is it that David, in the Spirit, called him Lord?" Jesus, who was a direct descendant of David, was at the same time, the Son of God. Everyone was confounded by this question. In fact, no one asked him any more questions that day. By posing it, Jesus again claimed to be God.

Response #2: "Woe to You, Hypocrites!" (#137a)

Matt 23:1–36
Mark 12:38–40
Luke 20:45–47

Addressing the people and his disciples, Jesus issued a series of scathing rebukes against the scribes and Pharisees. In Jesus' day, they were admired for their piety. Everyone must have been terribly shocked as Jesus repeated seven times, "Woe to you, scribes and Pharisees, hypocrites!" (Matt 23:13, 15, 16, 23, 25, 27, 29). At the end, there could be no doubt Jesus had denounced the religious leaders and their authority and replaced them with his own.

Response #3: Lament over Jerusalem (#137b)

Matt 23:37–39

Jesus loved people. He also knew the future. Knowing the city of Jerusalem was going to be destroyed broke his heart. While at the temple in Jerusalem, Jesus yet again began to weep for the city's destruction. It wouldn't take place for another 40 years, but Jerusalem's destruction will come because of the people's rejection of Jesus. As he did three months earlier (see Figure 54 on page 29), Jesus used similar language to describe his tender affection for the city.

> "How often would I have gathered your children together as a hen gathers her brood under her wings, and you were not willing!" (Matt 23:37; cf. Luke 13:34, #113b).

Response #4: The Widow's Two Mites (#138)

Mark 12:41–44
Luke 21:1–4

Jesus concluded his time at the temple by pointing out an example of pure religion. In the Court of the Women, there were 13 trumpet-shaped collection boxes. As many rich people put large amounts of coins in the treasury, a poor woman put in two bronze coins called leptons (meaning "small") or mites. They were hardly worth anything (1/128 of a denarius). Knowing this was all the money the woman possessed, Jesus praised her for her sacrifice, devotion, and pure religion. Her gift was sharply contrasted with the insincerity of the religious leaders' hypocrisy. "This poor widow," he said, "has put in more than all of them."

Matt 24–25
Mark 13
Luke 21:5–36

The Olivet Discourse (#139)

One of Jesus' longest speeches is the Olivet Discourse. He spoke these words from the Mount of Olives not far from Jerusalem. In it, Jesus predicted the destruction of Jerusalem at the hands of the Romans in A.D. 70.

The Olivet Discourse is also called the Eschatological (es-kuh-toe-LAW-juh-cool) Discourse because Jesus additionally spoke about the judgment of all the world at the end of time, an event we are still anticipating today. *Eschatology* is a technical term for "the end times" and the second coming of Jesus.

Matt 24:1–3
Mark 13:1–4
Luke 21:5–7

Setting of the Discourse (#139a)

Jesus and his apostles left the temple in Jerusalem and headed toward the Mount of Olives. As they left, several of the apostles turned to admire the large stones used to construct the temple grounds. Jesus then told them about the city's future demise: "Not one stone will be left upon another."

Stones that fell, or were pushed, from the Temple Mount to the street below in A.D. 70 at the time of the destruction by the Romans.

Shocked by this prediction, the apostles asked Jesus:

1. "When will these things be?" (#139b–e)
2. "What will be the sign of your coming and of the end of the age?" (#139e–g)

By asking the first question, they wanted to know when the destruction of Jerusalem would take place. The first half of the Olivet Discourse addressed this topic (Matt 24:4–35; Mark 13:5–31; Luke 21:28–33, #139b–e). The second question, which anticipated Jesus' reappearance at the end of time, was answered in the second half of the Olivet Discourse (Matt 24:36–25:46; Mark 13:32–37; Luke 21:34–36, #139e–g).

Matt 24:4–14
Mark 13:5–13
Luke 21:8–19

Beginning of Birth Pains (#139b)

Question #1: "When Will These Things Be?" The destruction of Jerusalem took place in A.D. 70, but tensions between the Jews and the Roman prefect, Gessius Florus, began in A.D. 66, surging into a Jewish revolt (*J.W.*, 2.14.5). Around this time, Rome itself was in turmoil as a result of the destructive rule of Emperor Nero and his suicide in A.D. 68. Over the next year and a half, three successive emperors failed to establish their rules (Tacitus, *Histories*, 1.2–3), until Vespasian seized control in A.D. 69. Several months later, he sent his son and future heir, Titus, to quash the Jewish rebellion.

In February of A.D. 70, Titus, the Roman general, surrounded Jerusalem with three legions of soldiers, sieging it until September of A.D. 70. The Jewish revolt continued several years, but was at last brought to a decisive and violent end. Jesus said this would be signaled by several signs he called "birth pains" (Figure 63).

The Siege and Destruction of Jerusalem by the Romans Under the Command of Titus, A.D. 70.

Painting by David Roberts (1850).

Three "Birth Pains" Before Jerusalem's Destruction

Signs	Citation
People claiming to be the Messiah (or Christ)	Matt 24:5
Wars and rumors of wars	Matt 24:6–7a
Famines and earthquakes	Matt 24:7b

Figure 63.

The first-century historian, Josephus, suggested that over a million Jews were killed by Titus and his Roman forces (*J.W.*, 6.9.3). While this figure was likely exaggerated, the destruction of Jerusalem was total and complete, including the beautiful Herodian temple.

By predicting these events beforehand, Jesus was giving his disciples an opportunity to anticipate Jerusalem's destruction and the violent persecution the Jewish people would endure. But they were not to sit idly by as the years unfolded: Jesus expected Christians to promote the church and share the gospel with as many people as they could.

> "And this gospel of the kingdom will be proclaimed throughout the whole world as a testimony to all nations, and then the end will come" (Matt 24:14).

Years before A.D. 70, the people living in the Mediterranean world had the chance to hear the gospel (1 Thess 1:8; Col 1:6, 23). Writing in late A.D. 57, the apostle Paul praised God for guiding the proclamation of the gospel "to all nations" (Rom 16:26; cf. Rom 1:5, 8).

> For not only has the word of the Lord sounded forth from you in Macedonia and Achaia, but your faith in God has gone forth everywhere, so that we need not say anything.
>
> —1 Thess 1:8

Matt 24:15–28
Mark 13:14–23
Luke 21:20–24

Abomination of Desolation (#139c)

The destruction of Jerusalem would not come unexpectedly. Jesus gave instructions to his disciples so they would know when it was time to flee for safety.

> "When you see the 'abomination of desolation' standing where he should not be . . ., then let those who are in Judea flee to the mountains" (Matt 24:15–16).

This phrase, "abomination of desolation," is from Daniel, the Old Testament prophet (Dan 9:27; 11:31; 12:11). Originally, it referred to Antiochus Epiphanes IV who desecrated the temple by erecting an altar to Zeus and sacrificing pigs (see page 19 of volume 1). Many believe Jesus was applying this phrase to the Roman general, Titus, who offered pagan sacrifices upon the temple's altar after the city's destruction (*J. W.* 6.316).

If this view is correct, then Jesus was not warning the citizens of *Jerusalem* to flee: By then, it would be too late, since the Roman army already would be inside the city. "Those who are in *Judea*," Jesus said, should hurriedly leave, praying for favorable conditions and not getting distracted while trying to flee (Figure 64).

Jesus' Instructions When Fleeing During the Destruction of Jerusalem

Instructions	Matthew	Mark	Luke
Hope you are not pregnant or nursing	Matt 24:19	Mark 13:17	Luke 21:23
Pray for favorable circumstances	Matt 24:20	Mark 13:18	—
Do not get distracted by false christs and false prophets	Matt 24:23–24	Mark 13:21–22	—

Figure 64.

Matt 24:29–31
Mark 13:24–27
Luke 21:25–27

Coming of the Son of Man (#139d)

Jesus used prophetic imagery to describe the destruction of Jerusalem. Similar words were used by several Old Testament prophets when predicting the fall of other enemy nations, including Babylon (Isa 13:10), Egypt (Ezek 32:7) and even Israel (Zech 12:10, 12–14). Allusions to the prophecies of Daniel continued when Jesus described the destruction of Jerusalem as the arrival of the "Son of Man coming on the clouds of heaven with power and glory." In the Old Testament vision, Daniel had seen "one like a son of man" approaching God, the Ancient of Days, and receiving an everlasting kingdom (Dan 7:13–14). Jesus is this "Son of Man."

There was more at stake than simply the punishment of Jerusalem: Jesus was vindicated when the city fell. By accurately predicting its destruction 40 years in advance, Jesus proved his claim to be "the Son of Man." The Jewish leadership should have listened to him and embraced him as the Messiah. Instead, they rejected him and were, in turn, punished by God.

> For the stars of the heavens and their constellations will not give their light; the sun will be dark at its rising, and the moon will not shed its light.
>
> —Isa 13:10

Signs of Nearness But Unknown Time (#139e, part 1)*

Matt 24:32–35
Mark 13:28–31
Luke 21:28–33

Jesus told a series of parables with the overriding themes of sudden judgment and the need for vigilance (Figure 65).

Parables in the Olivet Discourse

Parable	Matthew	Mark	Luke	Section
39. The Fig Tree	Matt 24:32–33	Mark 13:28–29	Luke 21:29–33	139e
40. The Owner of the House	Matt 24:42–44			139f
41. The Two Slaves	Matt 24:45–51			139f
42. The Wise and Foolish Virgins	Matt 25:1–13			139f
43. The Talents	Matt 25:14–30			139f
44. The Absent Master of the House		Mark 13:33–37		139f
45. The Sheep and the Goats	Matt 25:31–46			139g

Figure 65.

Parable of the Fig Tree

PARABLE 39 (see Sec. 109)
The Fig Tree

In the first parable, Jesus used the illustration of a fig tree. The leaves of a fig tree fall in the winter and new leaves begin to appear in the spring. When buds sprout on a fig tree, "you know that summer is near," Jesus said.

* Thomas and Gundry's *Harmony* does not make a break at Matt 24:36, choosing instead to extend #139e through Matt 24:41. I have divided #139 into two parts because, beginning in Matt 24:36, Jesus switched from talking about the destruction of Jerusalem (see Question #1 on page 72) to his second coming (see Question #2 on page 72). This is indicated by his switch from the plural "those days" (Matt 24:19, 22, 29) to the singular "that day" (Matt 24:36, 42, 50; 25:13). "Those days" refers to the destruction of Jerusalem and "that day" to the "end of the age."

In a similar way, the destruction of Jerusalem would be anticipated by Jesus' observant disciples. The Jewish wars of A.D. 66–70 pointed to God's eventual judgment on the city. Jesus—here in A.D. 30—predicted it would happen within 40 years when he said, "This generation will not pass away until all these things take place." He further emphasized its certainty by telling his disciples:

> "Heaven and earth will pass away, but my words will not pass away" (Matt 24:35).

There was no possible way Jesus' prediction would fail to occur.

Matt 24:36–41
Mark 13:32

Signs of Nearness But Unknown Time (#139e, part 2)

At this point in the Olivet Discourse, Jesus switched from talking about "these things" (Matt 24:3, 33–34) or "those days" (Matt 24:19, 22, 29) to "that day" (Matt 24:36, 42, 50; 25:13). This change signaled the end of Jesus' answer to the first question asked by the apostles and the beginning of his answer to the second (see the two questions listed on page 72). Jesus pivoted from talking about the destruction of Jerusalem to "the sign of [his] coming and the end of the age" (Matt 24:36).

Question #2: "What Will Be the Sign of Your Coming and of the End of the Age?" (Matt 24:36–25:46; Mark 13:32–37; Luke 21:34–36, #139e–g). While "birth pains" accompanied the destruction of Jerusalem (see Figure 63 on page 73), making it foreseeable, the arrival of Jesus cannot be predicted.

> "But concerning that day and hour no one knows, not even the angels of heaven, nor the Son, but the Father only" (Matt 24:36).

Remarkably, Jesus stated even he didn't know when his coming would be. He may be using hyperbole in order to emphasize the inability of anyone to know.

Because no signs point to the end, we must always be ready. But at the same time, we must live in the moment, taking nothing for granted. Jesus illustrated this by comparing "the end of the age" with Noah's day: Not knowing when the cataclysmic flood would occur, people were carrying on with their lives as normal.

Similarly, the destruction of Sodom and Gomorrah happened unexpectedly; Lot was able to escape only because of God's mercy.

Despite knowing everything could come to an end in an instant at any moment, our lives today should be characterized by a joy for living. Ultimately, we are never in total control of what happens to us, much less the end of the world. In light of this, we as disciples of Jesus should "endure to the end" (Mark 13:13, #139b).

Jesus also described two scenarios of sudden judgment.

- Two men will be farming in the field when one of them is suddenly taken.
- Two women will be grinding grain into flour at the village mill. Again, one of them will suddenly be taken.

Judgment will occur unexpectedly and suddenly, but not everyone will share the same fate. Those who are faithful to the end will be rewarded in judgment, the others will be "taken."

Parables on Watchfulness and Faithfulness (#139f)

Matt 24:42–25:30
Mark 13:33–37
Luke 21:34–36

Only the first Olivet Discourse parable (Parable 39, the Fig Tree) was used by Jesus to illustrate the destruction of Jerusalem. The remaining parables (Parables 40–45) applied to Jesus' return, an event that cannot be predicted (Matt 24:36). These parables also shared additional themes as well:

- The moment of the end is unknown and cannot be predicted.
- We must be ready at all times.
- Only those who are obedient will be saved.

Parable of the Owner of the House

PARABLE 40
The Owner of the House
Matt 24:42–44

Because thieves never advertise when they plan to burglarize a home, the owner of the house in this parable should always be prepared (cf. 1 Thess 5:2). We can never let up our guard because it will happen when we least expect it.

Parable of the Two Slaves

PARABLE 41
The Two Slaves
Matt 24:45–51

Two household slaves had been entrusted with caring for the other slaves while their master was away. The "faithful and wise servant" who performed his task was rewarded.

In sharp contrast with the "faithful and wise," the "wicked" slave took his master's delay as a license for irresponsible behavior. He not only disregarded his responsibilities, but abused those entrusted to his care. But the master returned suddenly when the wicked slave was unprepared. Those who live foolishly without regard for future judgment will suffer the same fate.

PARABLE 42
The Wise and Foolish Virgins
Matt 25:1–13

Parable of the Wise and Foolish Virgins

The important theme of delay introduced in the previous parable (Parable 41) was continued by Jesus in the next two (Figure 66). In the parable of the wise and foolish virgins, he compared the arrival of "the kingdom of heaven" to 10 virgins who were part of a village wedding procession. Five of these young ladies were "wise" and the remaining five were "foolish." What differentiated them was how they prepared for the happy couple's delay.

Theme of Delay in Parables 41–43

Parable	Jesus' Words in the Parable	Citation
41. The Two Slaves	"But if that wicked servant says to himself, 'My master is **delayed**'"…	Matt 24:48
42. The Wise and Foolish Virgins	"As the bridegroom was **delayed**, they all became drowsy and slept."	Matt 25:5
43. The Talents	"Now after a **long time** the master of those servants came and settled accounts with them."	Matt 25:19

Figure 66.

A vessel called an *askos* (which means "tube") was used as an oil container.

Throughout the evening, the wedding procession was marked by outdoor lamps that typically were made of cloths soaked in oil. As the night wore on, the oil was burned up, requiring more to be applied to the cloths.

The five wise virgins had brought an extra container of oil with them. But the five foolish virgins were in desperate need of more. "Give us some of your oil," they said to their friends, "for our lamps are going out" (v. 8). Unwilling to diminish their own supply by sharing, the "wise virgins" suggested the others go into the marketplace and buy additional oil. By the time they returned to the procession, the foolish virgins were too late: They missed the couple's arrival and the start of the wedding feast.

When they arrived at the house, the foolish virgins were prevented from entering (vv. 11–12; cf. Luke 13:25–27, #113a). Similarly, anyone who fails to always be prepared will find himself or herself on the outside looking in. "Watch therefore, for you know neither the day nor the hour," Jesus warned (v. 13).

Parable of the Talents

PARABLE 43 (see Sec. 127b)
The Talents
Matt 25:14–30

Three slaves were entrusted by their master with large sums of money called *talents*. While their master was away on a journey, they were expected to invest the money. Individual abilities determined the number of talents given to each slave. One received five talents to invest, another two, and the third slave received only one talent.

Talent

The largest unit of silver or gold equal to at least 10,000 denarii. (A denarius was a day's wage.)

The five- and two-talent slaves doubled their master's money and were praised for their successes. But the one-talent slave failed to do anything with his talent, instead choosing to bury it in the ground. Fear and laziness worked in tandem, paralyzing him from acting. As a result, the master punished him severely (v. 30).

Being the master's most productive investor, the five-talent slave who had made five additional talents received the one talent that had been hidden by the "wicked and slothful slave" (Figure 67). Jesus explained why this happened:

> "For to everyone who has will more be given, and he will have an abundance. But from the one who has not, even what he has will be taken away" (v. 29).

The Three Slaves in the Parable of the Talents

Original Amount Entrusted With	New Amount Entrusted With	Commendation Received from the Master	Citation
5 talents	11 talents	"Well done, good and faithful servant."	Matt 25:16, 20–21, 28
2 talents	4 talents	"Well done, good and faithful servant."	Matt 25:17, 22–23
1 talent	0 talents	"You wicked and slothful servant!"	Matt 25:18, 24–28

Figure 67.

God expects us to make use of the gifts and opportunities he has given us (cf. 1 Pet 4:10). Staying productive will help us stay alert.

PARABLE 44
The Absent Master of the House
Mark 13:33–37

Parable of the Absent Master of the House

This short parable emphasized the need to keep "awake." The reason why was because "the master of the house" could return at any time of day. Jesus used near identical phrases to emphasize the unpredictably of the Lord's return:

> "For you do not know when **the time** will come" (v. 33).
>
> "For you do not know when **the master** will come" (v. 35).

"Stay awake . . . lest [the master of the house] come suddenly and find you asleep" (v. 36), Jesus warned. We must not find ourselves asleep on the job and caught off guard when the end comes.

Matt 25:31–46

Judgment at the Son of Man's Coming (#139g)

In the final parable, Jesus fulfilled the prophet Daniel's vision. He is the "Son of Man" who has received "dominion and glory and a kingdom" (Dan 7:13–14). He will come "in his glory," accompanied by "all the angels," then "he will sit on his throne in glory and judge all the nations."

PARABLE 45
The Sheep and the Goats
Matt 25:31–46

Parable of the Sheep and the Goats

Just as a shepherd might separate his sheep from the goats, all the nations were divided into two groups before they were judged. King Jesus placed the righteous on his right side and the unrighteous on his left. From his throne, he addressed each group, calling the righteous those "who are blessed by my Father" and referring to the unrighteous as "you cursed ones." The difference between the righteous and the unrighteous revolved around how they treated others (Figure 68). "I was hungry," Jesus said, shocking both groups who thought Jesus was suggesting he had literally been seen in these various states of deprivation and need.

Contrast Between the Righteous and Unrighteous

The Righteous (vv. 35–36)	The Unrighteous (vv. 42–43)
"For I was hungry and you gave me food"	"For I was hungry and you gave me **no** food"
"I was thirsty and you gave me drink"	"I was thirsty and you gave me **no** drink"
"I was a stranger and you welcomed me"	"I was a stranger and you **did not** welcome me"
"I was naked and you clothed me"	"naked and you **did not** clothe me"
"I was sick and you visited me"	"sick [and you **did not** visit me]"
"I was in prison and you came to me"	"in prison and you **did not** visit me"

Figure 68.

Jesus was closely aligning himself with the poor and neglected. He further explained that when someone helped (or failed to help) "one of the least of these my brothers," it was as if he or she was helping (or neglecting) Jesus. The resulting judgments made a sharp contrast:

- The sheep were permitted to enter eternal life.
- The goats were doomed to eternal punishment.

How we treat others affects our soul's salvation (cf. 1 Pet 3:7). This is not to say our acts of charity are the exclusive means of determining where we will spend eternity. But they demonstrate the kind of hearts we have as citizens of Jesus' kingdom.

> "Husbands, live with your wives in an understanding way… **so that your prayers may not be hindered.**"
>
> —1 Pet 3:7

In the Olivet Discourse, Jesus warned his disciples to "stay awake" (Matt 24:42), "be ready" (Matt 24:44) and "watch" (Matt 25:13). The sense of urgency remains for us today as we await the return of King Jesus, too.

> But according to his promise we are waiting for new heavens and a new earth in which righteousness dwells. Therefore, beloved, since you are waiting for these, be diligent to be found by him without spot or blemish, and at peace (2 Pet 3:13–14).

Arrangements Made for Betrayal (#140, 142)

WEDNESDAY
Matt 26:1–5, 14–16
Mark 14:1–2, 10–11
Luke 22:1–6

By the end of Tuesday's disastrous confrontations with Jesus, the religious leaders—the chief priests, scribes, elders, Pharisees the Herodians—had failed in their attempts to discredit Jesus. These God-fearing religious leaders discussed among themselves how they would destroy Jesus.

With the Passover only two days away, thousands of extra people were in the city, many of whom respected Jesus as a prophet. Fearing the crowds, the religious leaders decided to wait until after the Passover and Feast of Unleavened Bread.

Sometime on Wednesday, they were approached by one of Jesus' own apostles. In exchange for 30 pieces of silver, Judas infamously agreed to deliver Jesus to them. They eagerly moved up their timetable and devised a sinister plan to murder Jesus.

THURSDAY, NISAN 14

Matt 26:17–29, 31–35
Mark 14:12–25, 27–31
Luke 22:7–38
John 13:1–38
1 Cor 11:23–26

The Last Supper (#143–148)

The Passover, which occurred on Thursday evening, commemorated the most significant event in Israelite history. In the Book of Exodus, the Israelites found themselves enslaved to the Egyptians. God remembered his covenant with Abraham and freed them by unleashing 10 devastating plagues on this powerful nation and its mighty Pharaoh (Ex 1–15).

The last plague God sent on Egypt was the death of the firstborn sons. But God provided a means of escape for the ancient Israelites. They were commanded by God through Moses to kill an unblemished one-year-old male lamb (Ex 12:1–28). Before roasting it, they were to take some of its blood and apply it to their doorposts before God came at midnight to kill all the firstborn sons. Any homes with the blood on the door's lintel would be *passed over* and those inside would be spared, thus the name, *Passover*. (See #31 on page 92 of volume 1.)

The Egyptians were not so fortunate. With this 10th and final plague—the death of the firstborn—God judged this oppressive nation and demonstrated his power over their false gods. Reeling from grief, Pharaoh and the Egyptians finally allowed the Israelites to leave. Soon afterwards, Israel entered into a covenant with God at Mt. Sinai (Ex 19:1–6), which included the Ten Commandments (Ex 20:1–21).

Since that original exodus from Egypt, the Jews celebrated the Passover every year. By now, they had observed this event and the seven-day Feast of Unleavened Bread that followed it for well over 1,000 years.* Over that period of time, many traditions crept into the observance that were not actually mentioned in the Mosaic Law. One included the singing of a hymn, which was what Jesus did with his apostles after they partook of the Passover meal (Matt 26:30; Mark 14:26). Often, people would sing some of the "hallelujah" psalms (Pss 113–118).

* The two events, Passover and the Feast of Unleavened Bread, were so entwined in their minds that the religious leaders will later refer to the Feast of Unleavened Bread as the Passover, later in John 18:28, #159).

Preparation for the Passover Meal (#143)

Matt 26:17–19
Mark 14:12–16
Luke 22:7–13

Jesus very much wanted to eat the Passover with his disciples (Luke 22:15). On Thursday morning, he sent Peter and John to someone's home in Jerusalem. The man was never named, but Jesus had foreseen that he would be carrying a jar of water. He told his two apostles to be on the lookout for this man. His home included a furnished upper room. Here, Peter and John prepared the Passover meal, which would have included the roasted lamb, bitter herbs, unleavened bread, and several servings of wine that were used as part of the Passover ceremony.

Jesus Washes the Disciples' Feet (#144–145)

Matt 26:20
Mark 14:17
Luke 22:14–16, 24–30
John 13:1–20

A Messianic fever had filled Jerusalem. Jesus had never been more popular with the people. Having been with Jesus now over three years, the apostles believed he was destined for greatness. After this week's events, they had a sense that something momentous was going to happen soon. The apostles, like most of the people, believed Jesus as the Messiah would establish an earthly kingdom and rule Jerusalem as David's rightful heir.

As they sat at the table, their conversations with one another quickly turned into an argument over who was the greatest among them. This was, unfortunately, not the first time they had vied for positions of authority in Jesus' kingdom (Figure 69).

The Bickering of the Apostles over Greatness in Christ's Kingdom

Description	Citation	Section
They were indignant with James and John when they requested positions of prominence in his kingdom	Mark 9:33–34; Luke 9:46–48	#90
They argued with one another about who was the greatest	Matt 20:20–28	#125b
They argued yet again with one another over who was the greatest	Luke 22:24–30	#144

Figure 69.

Jesus loved these men dearly. But how it must have frustrated him to see their immaturity on full display on the eve of his death. In response, he quietly got up from the table and began to remove his outer clothing. He came back holding a basin of water with a towel wrapped around his waist.

He looked like a household slave.

A hushed silence must have come over the room as they saw what he was doing. An uncomfortable feeling no doubt overwhelmed their hearts as Jesus proceeded to wash their feet. He came up to each one and removed his sandals. Jesus then performed the lowly task of washing the disciples' feet. When it was Peter's turn, the apostle objected to his feet being washed by Jesus.

> Peter said to him, "You shall never wash my feet." Jesus answered him, "If I do not wash you, you have no share with me" (John 13:8).

Peter then asked Jesus to wash his hands and head as well. Jesus responded with somber words about Judas, who would betray him later that evening.

> Jesus said to him, "The one who has bathed does not need to wash, except for his feet, but is completely clean. And you are clean, but not every one of you" (John 13:10).

Still in the room, Judas had seen all the miracles and heard all the wonderful lessons that Jesus had taught. And yet when he saw this incredible display of humility, he still was determined to proceed with the betrayal.

Matt 26:21–25
Mark 14:18–21
Luke 22:21–23
John 13:21–30

The Betrayer is Identified (#146)

After teaching them about humility by washing their feet, Jesus went back to his place at the table. Then, he grew visibly upset. "One of you is going to be betray me," he said. The disciples began looking at one another, wondering to whom Jesus was referring. None of them seem to have even suspected it was Judas.

They began one by one asking Jesus, "Surely not I, Lord?" Judas also took his turn and brazenly asked, "Surely not I, Rabbi?" Jesus knew, and Judas knew. The others were oblivious.

According to John 13:23–25, John and Judas were sitting on either side of Jesus.* We know this because John, the disciple "whom Jesus loved," is described as "reclining at table at Jesus' side" and then "leaning back against Jesus." As was customary in the first century, they were reclined at a low table lying on pillows. Peter motioned to John to ask Jesus who it was he was talking about.

> Jesus answered, "It is he to whom I will give this morsel of bread when I have dipped it." So when he had dipped the morsel, he gave it to Judas, the son of Simon Iscariot (John 13:26).

As Judas ate the morsel, Jesus said to him, "What you do, do quickly." And with that, Judas left the company of his former friends and walked into the darkness outside.

Jesus Predicts Peter's Denial (#147)

Matt 26:31–35
Mark 14:27–31
Luke 22:31–38
John 13:31–38

The week had started out so promisingly, but during the Passover meal on Thursday night, it took an ominous turn. It got worse when Jesus told them he was leaving them, and they wouldn't be able to follow him just yet (John 13:36). Then he added: "This very night you will all fall away on account me" (Matt 26:31).

Peter would have none of this. "Even if all fall away on account of you, I never will," he said in defiance of Jesus' prediction. As the others chimed in and said the same thing, Jesus focused on Peter and uttered these words:

> "Peter, the rooster will not crow this day, until you deny three times that you know me" (Luke 22:34).

Peter contradicts Jesus once again.

> Peter said to him, "Even if I must die with you, I will not deny you!" And all the disciples said the same (Matt 26:35).

Despite their protestations, the apostles fled when Jesus was arrested in only a few hours (Matt 26:56, #153, page 281). Everything happened just as Jesus had said it would.

---

* Sitting next to Jesus would have been a great honor for Judas and John. Jesus was likely trying to persuade Judas to back out of his plans to betray him by seating his betrayer right next to him during the Last Supper.

Matt 26:26–29
Mark 14:22–25
Luke 22:17–20
1 Cor 11:23–26

Jesus Institutes the Lord's Supper (#148)

When Jesus ate the Passover with his apostles that night, he did something else with them as well. He instituted a new memorial meal that would be later called "the Lord's Supper" (1 Cor 11:20).

This new observance anticipated Jesus' sacrificial death. Using two Passover elements, Jesus took unleavened bread and "the fruit of the vine" and gave them new meaning (see Figure 70).

> Now as they were eating, Jesus took bread, and after blessing it broke it and gave it to the disciples, and said, "Take, eat; this is my body." And he took a cup, and when he had given thanks he gave it to them, saying, "Drink of it, all of you, for this is my blood of the covenant, which is poured out for many for the forgiveness of sins (Matt 26:26–28).

The passover celebration included four cups of wine that commemorated the covenant. Jesus used one of these cups when he instituted the Lord's Supper and established the new covenant in his blood.

The broken pieces of unleavened bread represented the broken body of Jesus. Although none of his bones were broken, his flesh would be torn to shreds by the brutal scourging and the nails used to secure him to the cross. The fruit of the vine represented his blood that he shed. Jesus went on to add that this is a memorial feast to be observed until he returns.

Passover and the Lord's Supper Contrasted

Passover	Lord's Supper
Celebrated freedom from Egyptian slavery	Celebrated freedom from sin
Israel was freed in order to establish a covenant with God	Jesus freed us and established a new covenant (Luke 22:20)
Participants ate the Passover lamb, bitter herbs, unleavened bread and drank wine	Participants eat unleavened bread and drink fruit of the vine which represent Jesus' blood
The blood of the Passover lamb was shed	The blood of Jesus was shed (1 Cor 5:7; John 1:29, 36)
Observed once a year	Observed once a week (cf. Acts 20:7)

Figure 70.

The Lord's Supper was observed by first-century Christians every Sunday (cf. Acts 20:7). The apostle Paul emphasized its importance when he repeated the institution of the Lord's Supper in 1 Cor 11:23–26. To this day, on each Sunday, we reflect on Jesus' four statements when he instituted the Lord's Supper.

- "This is my body."
- "This is my blood of the covenant, which is poured out for many."
- "Do this in remembrance of me."
- "I will never again drink of the fruit of the vine until that day when I drink it new in the kingdom of God."

When we eat the Lord's Supper, we are eating with Jesus. Although he is not physically present, he is spiritually with us. We are eating and drinking with Jesus as we renew our commitment to him.

The Farewell Discourse (#149–150)

John 14–16

John 13–17 (#145–147, 149–151) is called the Farewell Discourse or the Upper Room Discourse. Even though he knew he was going to be betrayed later that night, Jesus wanted to spend this precious time impressing several themes upon the minds of his 11 apostles (Judas had departed the room, John 13:30).

- Jesus is one with God. They would be able to find peace by renewing their relationship with him and the Father.
- Jesus must leave them, but will send the Holy Spirit to help them.
- Love, unity, and joy will characterize how true disciples interact with each other.
- Jesus' followers will suffer persecution from the world.

Farewell Discourses

A literary form in which a leader leaves instructions to his followers.

There are several examples of farewell discourses in the Bible.

- Jacob (Gen 47:29–49:33)
- Moses (Deut 1–33)
- Joshua (Josh 22–24)
- David (1 Chron 28–29)
- Jesus (John 13–17)
- Paul (Acts 20:17–38)

These ideas recurred throughout the following divisions of the Farewell Discourse. Only after the death, burial, and resurrection of Jesus would his apostles begin to fully understand what he meant by these important words (cf. John 2:22, #31).

Questions about His Destination, the Father, and the Holy Spirit Answered (#149)

John 14:1–31

Prior to instituting the Lord's Supper, Jesus told his apostles he was leaving them and they couldn't come with him right now.

> "Where I am going you cannot follow me now, but you will follow afterward" (John 13:36, #147).

"The Way"

"The way" occurs three times in John 14:4–6.

Jesus: "You know **the way**."

Thomas: "How can we know **the way**?"

Jesus: "I am **the way**…"

> Jesus said to them, "I am the way, and the truth, and the life. No one comes to the Father except through me."
>
> —John 14:6

This is one of the most famous statements of Jesus from his Farewell Discourse.

When they next heard Jesus predict Peter's upcoming denials (John 13:37–38, #147), their faces must have revealed their surprise. But then Jesus said, "Let not your hearts be troubled. Believe in God, believe also in me" (John 14:1). In other words, Jesus was telling them, "Trust me!"

He gently explained the reason he had to leave them: "I go to prepare a place for you" (v. 2). But the idea they would be without Jesus' physical presence confused them and left them brokenhearted. "You know the way," he assured them, as he explained they all would be reunited one day.

> Thomas said to him, "Lord, we do not know where you are going. How can we know the way?" Jesus said to him, "I am the way, and the truth, and the life. No one comes to the Father except through me" (John 14:5–6).

These magnificent words summarized Jesus' entire ministry. He came to blaze the trail that would lead us all to God, the Father. This *way* is the only true way and leads to eternal life.

Philip asked him to reveal the Father to them. But Jesus insisted he already had, "Whoever has seen me has seen the Father." God the Father and Jesus the Son are one in their essence (cf. John 10:30, #111). Jesus then promised to send them the Holy Spirit, who shares their divine essence (cf. Col 2:9; cf. Matt 28:19, #181).

> "And I will ask the Father, and he will give you another Helper, to be with you forever, even the Spirit of truth, whom the world cannot receive, because it neither sees him nor knows him. You know him, for he dwells with you and will be in you" (John 14:16–17; see also John 16:7, #150c).

This word *helper* is difficult to translate. Sometimes, it is rendered in our English translations as "comforter," "counselor," "advocate" or even *Paraclete* (pronounced PAIR-uh-cleet, a term derived from the Greek word).

Notice that Jesus referred to the Holy Spirit as "another" comforter or helper who would provide what they lacked in themselves as Jesus' ambassadors to the world. In other words, Jesus had been their first "helper" (cf. 1 John 2:1). Both Jesus and the Holy Spirit were sent by God to assist the apostles and their associates as they spread the gospel. In his last moments with them, Jesus told his apostles his mission would continue, even after he left and returned to the Father, by the acts of the Holy Spirit.

The Vine and the Branches (#150a)

John 15:1–17

In addition to his union with the Father and the Holy Spirit, Jesus stressed the living relationship he had with the disciples. He compared this connection to a farmer and his vineyard.

> "I am the true vine, and my Father is the vinedresser. . . . You are the branches" (John 15:1, 5).

Disciples connected to Jesus would thrive and bear fruit. Although these words are specifically directed to the 11 apostles, a broader application may be made. Spiritual productivity is not due to a Christian's abilities, but because of his or her connection with God. Jesus emphasized the importance of "abiding" or "remaining" in him (vv. 4–7) and in his love (vv. 9–10). This reciprocal relationship would continue to exist even after Jesus returned to the Father (cf. John 14:19–20, #149).

In the Old Testament, Israel and its relationship with God was often compared with a gardener and his vineyard (cf. Isa 5:1–2).

Jesus also connected his love for the disciples with their joy in him (v. 11). Remaining in Jesus' love means to delight in a living relationship with him every day, being completely dependent on the "true vine" (v. 1) as the source of complete joy.

Earlier in the Farewell Discourse, Jesus spoke of the importance of not only abiding in his love, but also of his disciples loving one another.

> "A new commandment I give to you, that you love one another: just as I have loved you, you also are to love one another. By this all people will know that you are my disciples, if you have love for one another" (John 13:34–35, #147).

This commandment is repeated in John 15:12. And then, Jesus cited his sacrifice on the cross as the ultimate display of love.

> "Greater love has no one than this, that someone lay down his life for his friends. You are my friends if you do what I command you" (John 15:13).

This sacrificial love served as the foundation for the apostles' relationship with God and other disciples. Similarly, everything we do must be motivated by the selfless love. When we abide in Jesus, our service to others will show people we are Jesus' friends.

John 15:18–16:4

Opposition From the World (150b)

The antithesis of love is hate. The world, Jesus said, hated him and, as a result, would hate his disciples, too. The reason for this hatred was unwarranted, of course (v. 25). Jesus loved the world and sacrificed himself for the very people who wanted to destroy him (cf. John 3:16, #32b).

Earlier in his ministry, Jesus had warned the disciples of the severe persecutions they would face as they preached (Matt 10:16–19, #70b). But they would have assistance from the "helper" (vv. 26–27). In the Book of Acts, the Holy Spirit guided them in their preaching, filling them with courage to face the religious leaders and proclaim the truth, despite the consequences (cf. Acts 4:31).

John 16:5–15

The Coming and Ministry of the Spirit (150c)

Jesus told his apostles it was absolutely necessary for him to leave so the Holy Spirit could be sent in his place. During their ministries, the apostles were inspired by the Holy Spirit to preach the gospel (cf. Mark 13:11, #139). He would inspire eight men to write the New Testament, including four of the apostles (Matthew, John, Peter, and Paul). These inspired authors "spoke from God as they were carried along by the Holy Spirit" (2 Pet 1:21).

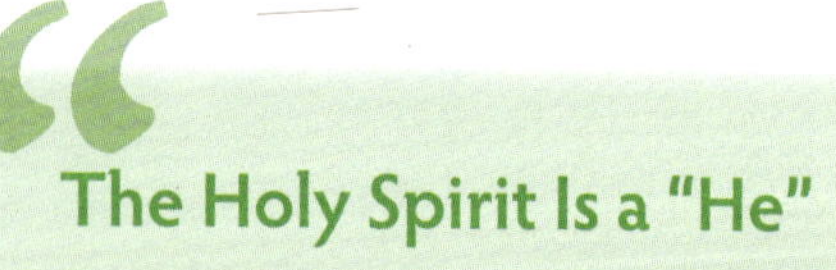

The Holy Spirit Is a "He"

"When the Spirit of truth comes, **he** will guide you into all truth..."

—John 16:13

In Greek, the word "spirit" is neuter in gender. But because the Holy Spirit is not an "it," Jesus uses a masculine pronoun in reference to him.

The Holy Spirit's ministry would also include convicting the world for killing Jesus (Figure 71). The religious leaders sinned by refusing to believe in Jesus (v. 9), crucifying him instead. In turn, Jesus would be vindicated when he was raised from the dead and ascended to the Father, evident by the fact his disciples would "see [Jesus] no longer" (v. 10). And finally, judgment was certain because the devil, "the ruler of this world," had been defeated by Jesus through his resurrection and ascension (v. 11; cf. Heb 2:14).

The Holy Spirit's Ministry to the World

Message	Explanation	Citation
Sin	The world refused to believe in Jesus	John 16:9
Righteousness	Jesus was vindicated (declared righteous) by his ascension	John 16:10
Judgment	Jesus defeated Satan, "the ruler of this world" (cf. Heb 2:14)	John 16:11

Figure 71.

Unlike the world, the disciples did believe in Jesus and now knew where he was going. Hard as it might be for them to live without the presence of their friend and Lord, they knew Jesus was the Messiah whose mission had been to defeat Satan.

Prediction of Joy Over His Resurrection (#150d)

John 16:16–22

Jesus' 3½-year ministry was quickly drawing to a close. Time was running out—and he knew it. Despite hearing these predictions to the contrary, Jesus' apostles refused to believe he was about to be murdered. And so, when Jesus said, "A little while, and you will not see me," they were perplexed and confused.

He told them that they would experience deep sorrow upon his death, but it would soon turn into joy when he was resurrected. Just as a mother's terrible pain during childbirth gives way to joy when the baby is delivered, so also would the disciples suffer and then rejoice when Jesus lived again. "And no one will take your joy from you," he said.

In his illustration about the mother giving birth, Jesus said, "she has sorrow because *her hour has come*" (v. 21). He likely was making reference to his own "hour." Throughout his ministry, he had said repeatedly "my hour has not yet come" (John 2:4; 7:30; 8:20). That now had changed (John 12:23, #130a).

The hour for him to "depart out of this world" and glorify God had arrived (John 13:1, #145; 17:1, #151). Jesus' betrayal and crucifixion were right around the corner (Lesson 13).

John 16:23–33

Promise of Answered Prayer and Peace (150e)

"In that day," that is, after Jesus' resurrection, the disciples would understand everything he had been saying to them about himself and the purpose of his ministry. With the assistance of the Holy Spirit, they would no longer need to ask him questions. That's one major change soon to take place.

> For there is one God, and there is one mediator between God and men, the man Christ Jesus.
>
> —1 Tim 2:5

Whether or not we say the words, "In Jesus' name...," every pray we offer to God is through Jesus, our intercessor.

But another was how they should pray. After his resurrection and ascension, Jesus wanted his disciples to begin praying in his name (cf. John 14:13, #149). Even now, Jesus Christ serves as our mediator: We have direct access to God through our high priest, Jesus (1 Tim 2:5; Heb 4:14–16).

Jesus then told them plainly what was about to happen:

> "I came from the Father and have come into the world, and now I am leaving the world and going to the Father" (v. 28).

Jesus' mission was to seek and save the lost (cf. Luke 19:10, #127a). At this point in the Farewell Discourse, the apostles responded favorably to Jesus' openness about the changes taking place soon. And then, he became even more plain with them, reminding them of his prediction that they would all forsake him.

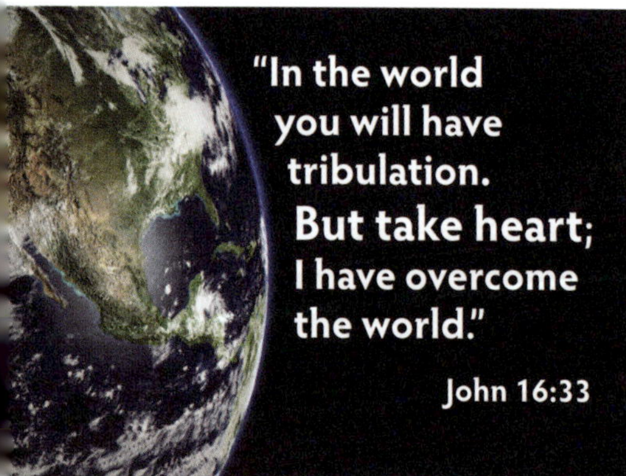

> "Behold, the hour is coming, indeed it has come, when you will be scattered, each to his own home, and will leave me alone. Yet I am not alone, for the Father is with me. I have said these things to you, that in me you may have peace. In the world you will have tribulation. But take heart; I have overcome the world" (vv. 32–33).

"I have overcome the world." They needed to hear these words, since they would soon suffer opposition from the world (John 15:20). In the Book of Acts, the apostles risked everything to preach Jesus to those who murdered him (Acts 2:37; 3:13; 4:11–12).

Jesus had spoken of "my peace" (John 14:27), "my love" (John 15:9), and "my joy" (John 15:11). With his betrayal on his mind, Jesus spoke of triumph and victory. And he wants us also today to live with hope (Col 1:27; Titus 2:13), calm assurance (Eph 3:11–12; Heb 10:19), and peace (Phil 4:7; Col 3:15) reigning in our hearts.

Jesus' High Priestly Prayer (#151)

John 17

Throughout his ministry, Jesus prayed frequently (see Figure 51 on page 12), but all the words of his prayers are not recorded in the Gospels. Jesus offered a beautiful prayer in John 17 sometimes referred to as the High Priestly Prayer.* The importance of this prayer is evidenced by its completeness. In Jesus' longest-recorded prayer, he asked for:

- his own glorification (vv. 1–5),
- the ministry of his apostles (vv. 6–19), and
- "those who will believe in me through their word" (vv. 20–26).

"And now, Father, glorify me in your own presence with the glory that I had with you before the world existed."

—John 17:5

Jesus shared in the glory of God with God the Father and God the Holy Spirit before the creation of the material world.

With his ministry nearly fulfilled, Jesus was ready for the final step, by which God would glorify his Son. This would be accomplished by Jesus' death, resurrection, and exaltation. Everything had been leading up to this moment.

Jesus mentioned "the world" in his prayer 18 times. Most of these weren't about the physical earth (as in vv. 5, 15, 24), but expressed his deep concern for the people of the world who had yet to believe in him (cf. John 3:16, #32b). Jesus' intercession for the ministry of the apostles had two purposes: the unity of all believers and the salvation of the world (Figure 72).

The Purpose of the Apostles' Future Ministry

Benefit for Future Disciples	Benefit for the World	Citation
that **they** may all be **one**… that **they** also may be [**one**] in us,	so that the **world** may believe that you have sent me.	John 17:21
that **they** may be **one** even as we are **one**, that **they** may become perfectly **one**,	so that the **world** may know that you sent me and loved them even as you loved me.	John 17:22–23

Figure 72.

As God's high priest, Jesus made appeals to his Father on behalf of the entire world. Even though the world hated Jesus and his followers (v. 15), he wanted—and still wants—everyone to know and experience the love of God (vv. 25–26).

---

* The High Priestly Prayer is also referred to as the Farewell Prayer. In the Gospel of John, it serves as the conclusion to the entire Farewell Discourse (John 13–17, #145–147, 149–151).

Matt 26:30, 36–46
Mark 14:26, 32–42
Luke 22:39–46
John 18:1

Three Prayers on the Mount of Olives (#152)

The city of Jerusalem is 2,500 feet above sea level, higher than anything else in the area, with one exception. The Mount of Olives, located just east of the city, is 2,600 feet above sea level. It afforded a beautiful view of Jerusalem and of the magnificent Herodian temple. The visitor from the east would descend the mountain, cross the Kidron Valley, and then enter the temple area through the beautiful Golden Gate.

At the bottom of the Mount of Olives was an olive grove called the Garden of Gethsemane. In Jesus' day, it was a secluded and remote, walled garden. (Jesus "entered and "went out" of it.) He

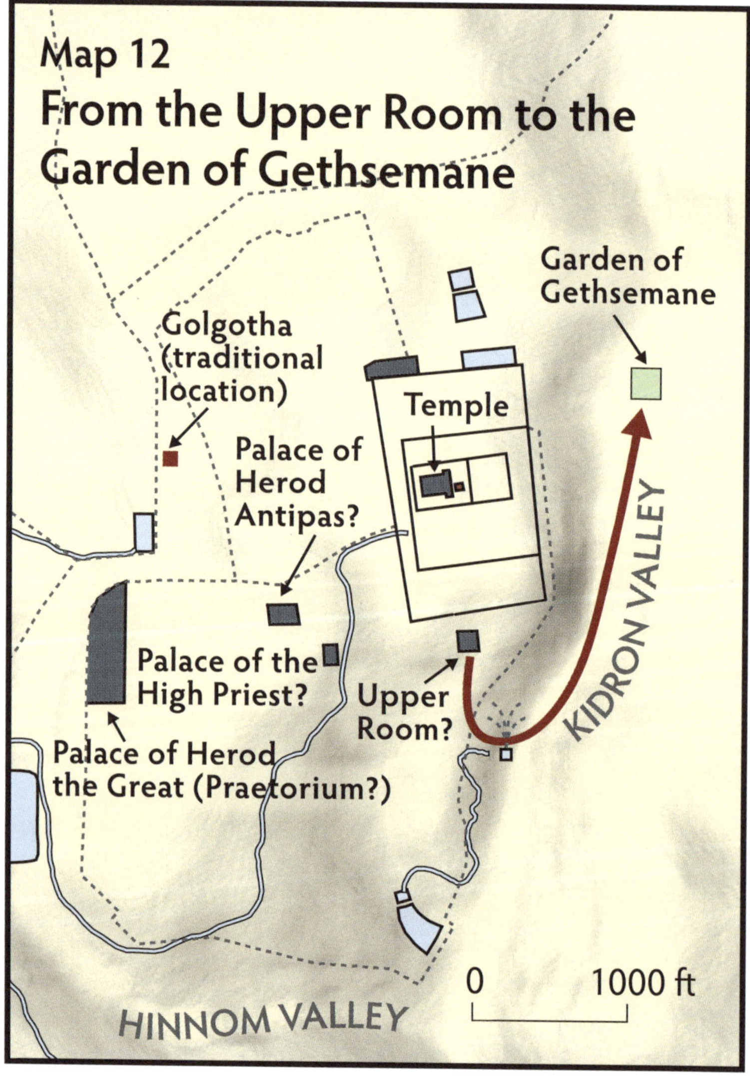

frequently prayed in it, sometimes spending all night in prayer (Luke 21:37). Anytime Jesus was near the city of Jerusalem, he seems to have made his way to this favorite location. Jesus also spent many hours there with his apostles, teaching them. Jesus loved to spend time in the garden to rest and meditate. He normally felt safe there.

Tonight, he wasn't safe. And, he knew it.

For three years, Jesus had been saying, "My hour has not yet come." Now it had come (John 17:1, #151). The moment was upon him. Anticipation of the pain and anguish he would soon endure engulfed his mind. On this fateful night, he was in emotional turmoil. Bent over with his face near the ground, Jesus prayed the same agonizing prayer three separate times.

> "My Father, if it be possible, let this cup pass from me; nevertheless, not as I will, but as you will" (Matt 26:39; Luke 22:42).

An angel appeared, strengthening Jesus (Luke 22:43). Angels had similarly helped Jesus after his temptation in the wilderness (Matt 4:11, #25). Jesus knew how grueling the crucifixion was going to be. The very fact Jesus needed encouragement in the face of

Gethsemane

Gethsemane in Hebrew means "olive press."

The Garden of Gethsemane was located at the bottom of the Mount of Olives.

Edward Lear's painting (1858),
Jerusalem from the Mount of Olives at Sunrise

trials should bring comfort to us. Because the sinless Son of God struggled with anguish, we should not expect our experiences to be any different.

His feelings were so intense he began to sweat like drops of blood (Luke 22:44). This may be describing hematidrosis, a rare medical condition in which tiny capillaries in the sweat glands break, causing bloody sweat. This condition is brought on by extreme stress or fear, the kind of mental anguish Jesus was under as he anticipated his impending death on the cross.

Jesus was not the only person overcome with emotion that night. His three closest apostles—Peter, James, and John—had accompanied him to this part of the garden. Seemingly oblivious to Jesus' emotional struggles, however, they struggled with fatigue and sorrow, unable to keep their eyes open. Jesus rebuked them because they could not stay awake with him.

> "So, could you not watch with me one hour? . . . The spirit indeed is willing, but the flesh is weak" (Matt 26:40–41).

And then, suddenly he said, "Rise, let us be going; my betrayer is at hand!" (Matt 26:46; Mark 14:42).

The garden was then flooded with a large group of armed Roman soldiers. Their flaming torches filled the garden with light, even as the forces of darkness descended upon it.

Conclusion

Throughout the final week, Jesus was always keenly aware he had only a few days to spend with his apostles. He needed them to understand *before* he died that his death was part of the divine plan of God. Even though he had told them repeatedly he was going to Jerusalem to die, Jesus knew they would not accept it.

The anointing of Jesus by Mary was the first in a series of events that culminated in Jesus' death on the cross. When Jesus' violent crucifixion happened, the disciples were caught off guard, despite the warnings from Jesus. But he knew it was time for the greatest event in human history to transpire—Jesus' hour had come.

WHAT DID YOU LEARN IN LESSON 12?

Match the key concept in the numbered list below with the letter of the phrase that best describes it. Answers appear upside-down at the bottom of the page.

Key Concepts

1. Mount of Olives
2. Triumphal Entry
3. Basin of water
4. Passion
5. Lord's Supper
6. Gethsemane
7. Upper Room
8. Hosanna
9. Lepton
10. Spikenard
11. Helper
12. Last Supper

Descriptions

A. A small Roman coin sometimes called a mite. Two of these coins were contributed to the temple by a poor widow.

B. A term that describes the role of both Jesus and the Holy Spirit in the future ministries of the apostles.

C. The term used to describe Jesus' arrival into Jerusalem on the Sunday before his crucifixion.

D. A very expensive ointment imported from India used by Mary to anoint Jesus.

E. The garden at the bottom of the Mount of Olives where Jesus was betrayed and arrested.

F. The term used by the crowds as Jesus entered Jerusalem riding on the foal of a donkey. It means, "Save us."

G. What Jesus used to wash the feet of his disciples.

H. A mountain east of Jerusalem known for its olive groves.

I. The final observance of the Passover by Jesus before his crucifixion.

J. A term from the Latin root "to suffer." It is often used to describe the last week of Jesus' life before his crucifixion.

K. The location in Jerusalem where Jesus met with his disciples on the night of his arrest.

L. The memorial Jesus established with his disciples as part of his new covenant on the night he was betrayed.

Answers

1H, 2C, 3G, 4J, 5L, 6E, 7K, 8F, 9A, 10D, 11B, 12I

WHAT DID YOU LEARN IN LESSON 12?

Do your best to answer the following questions. Some answers can be found in the text of Lesson 12, but not all of them. For others, you will be asked to look up passages in your Bible to find them.

Fill in the Blanks.

1. As Jesus entered the city of Jerusalem, what two items did people spread on the road in front of him (Matt 21:8, #128b)?

   ____

   ____

   Why did they do this? ______________________________

   ____

   ____

2. What did Jesus say were the two greatest commandments (Matt 22:37–39, #135)?

   1. Love ______________________________

   2. Love ______________________________

3. What was Jesus' "new commandment" to his disciples (John 13:34, #147)? ______________________________

   ____

4. What word did Jesus call the Pharisees and scribes (Matt 23:1–36, #137a)? ____________ What does it mean?

   ____

5. According to Jesus (Matt 24:36), who is the only person who knows when the end of the age will be? ____________

6. What special meal was Jesus eating with his disciples when he instituted the Lord's Supper? ____________

   ____

Multiple Choice. Circle the correct answer.

1. What did the religious leaders consider doing after Jesus raised Lazarus from the dead (John 12:9–11, #128a)?
   A. Become disciples of Jesus.
   B. Get Lazarus to take a DNA test to prove it was really him.
   C. Bribe Lazarus to betray Jesus.
   D. Murder Lazarus.

2. What did Mary anoint Jesus with?
   A. Soap and water.
   B. Spikenard.
   C. Olive oil.
   D. Canola oil.

3. Jesus made his entry into Jerusalem riding on . . .
   A. A horse.
   B. A donkey.
   C. A mule.
   D. Nothing. He walked, like he always did.

4. When he cleansed the temple, what two Old Testament prophets did Jesus quote from (Mark 11:17, #129b)?
   A. Isaiah and Jeremiah.
   B. Ezekiel and Daniel.
   C. Hosea and Amos.
   D. Zechariah and Malachi.

5. Some of the Jewish authorities believed in Jesus. Why did they not confess their faith in him (John 12:42–43, #130b)?
   A. They were afraid of being thrown out of the synagogue.
   B. They loved the praise of people more than of God.
   C. They might lose their jobs if they did.
   D. All the above.

6. Which apostle at first refused to let Jesus wash his feet?
   A. Peter.
   B. John.
   C. Philip.
   D. Judas.

APPLICATION OF LESSON 12.

For Discussion.

1. The concepts of suffering and glory are in constant tension throughout Jesus' ministry (cf. 1 Pet 1:11). Suffering must follow glory. Why? ______________________________

2. What does it mean that the two greatest commandments "depend on the Law and the Prophets" (Matt 22:37–39, #135)?

3. If the second coming of Jesus is unknowable (cf. Matt 24:36), then why do people try to predict the end of the world?

4. Why do you think Judas was so upset when Mary used expensive ointment to anoint Jesus (#141)? ______________

5. List reasons why people today refuse to confess their faith in Jesus to be the Christ, the Son of God (cf. John 12:42–43).

LESSON 13

Jesus on Trial (#153–161)

Matt 26:47–27:26
Mark 14:43–15:15
Luke 22:47–23:25
John 18:2–19:16a
Acts 1:18–19

Jesus' entire ministry culminated in the crucifixion. This single event motivated him to do everything up to this point. Now that the moment was upon him, anticipation of the pain and anguish he would soon endure engulfed his mind. But he was determined to die for the sins of all humanity. This was why he had come. And this was why he was going to allow himself to be killed by his enemies.

Betrayal and Arrest (#153)

FRIDAY
Matt 26:47–56
Mark 14:43–52
Luke 22:47–53
John 18:2–12

Jesus loved the garden of Gethsemane and frequented it often. His apostles, including Judas, were quite familiar with the garden. Judas, accompanied by a large group of Roman soldiers, temple guards and religious leaders, arrived at the garden just as Jesus was finishing his heart-wrenching prayer. This formidable group of armed men holding torches and lanterns surrounded Jesus and his small group of scared, defenseless apostles.

Jesus was not frightened. Instead, he calmly asked them, "Whom are you looking for?" They answered, "Jesus of Nazareth." His response was simple: "I am." Suddenly, as if knocked over by the power of these words, the Roman soldiers lost their footing and started falling backward toward the ground (John 18:6).

In the midst of this commotion, Jesus repeated his question. Again, they answered, "Jesus of Nazareth." Jesus rebuked them for coming after him under the cover of darkness. He agreed to go peacefully with them, but demanded his apostles go free.

Kiss of Betrayal

Judas walked up to Jesus and said, "Hail, Rabbi!" After greeting him in this way, he kissed Jesus on the cheek. This would have been the common greeting among friends, but tonight, it served as a signal to the soldiers who accompanied him. The kiss was a predetermined signal to clearly identify Jesus as the one they were there to apprehend (Matt 26:48; Mark 14:44).

Looking at his former apostle, Jesus asked, "Judas, would you betray the Son of Man with a kiss?" (Luke 22:48). He had known this was going to happen (cf. John 6:70–71). Tonight was the night he was betrayed by one of his own.

Jesus Arrested

The Roman short sword (gladius) would have measured 24–33" in length, 2–2.8" in width and weighed approximately 2 lbs.

Peter was not willing to give up without a fight though. Having been roused from his sleep, he no doubt was sluggish and reactionary. Even as another disciple started to ask Jesus if they should fight back, Peter pulled out a sword and attacked. In the face of such overwhelming odds, it was ridiculous to think they could overpower the Roman soldiers surrounding them and save Jesus.

As a result of his violent swishing of the sword, Peter cut off the right ear of Malchus, the high priest's slave. Rather than applaud his apostle's actions, Jesus scolded him. "Put your sword away!" he told Peter. "Shall I not drink the cup that the Father has given me?" (John 18:11). He then added:

> "Do you think that I cannot appeal to my Father, and he will at once send me more than twelve legions of angels?" (Matt 26:53).

MIRACLE 37
Restoring Malchus' Ear

Ever in control of the situation, Jesus healed Malchus' injury. Ironically, Jesus' last miracle assisted someone participating in his arrest. By turning the other cheek, Jesus showed everyone he meant what he had said repeatedly about the importance of forgiveness.

With his mind steeled for what was coming next, Jesus then allowed himself to be arrested. Jesus resolved to go with his captors, knowing these events were fulfillment of Scripture and would lead to his death.

Even though they had been told this numerous times, the apostles refused to accept the necessity of Jesus' death. Powerless to stop it, his terrified disciples fled the scene as the powers of darkness enveloped Jesus and carried him away to stand trial.

The four Gospels present a Jewish Trial and a Roman Trial with three phases each. The Jewish Trial took place first, quickly followed by the Roman Trial. The Jews wanted Jesus killed by crucifixion, but only the Roman governor of Judea could sentence Jesus to death by crucifixion. Before they delivered Jesus to Pilate, the Jewish leadership had to go through the motions of determining Jesus' guilt or innocence before formally charging him.

The Jewish Trial (#154–158)

Matt 26:57–27:26
Mark 14:53–15:15
Luke 22:54a–23:25
John 18:13–19:16a
Acts 1:18–19

The nation of Israel enjoyed the most advanced judicial system the world had ever known. In fact, many modern court systems are based on its principles. Under the Law of Moses, people were assumed innocent until proven guilty. It demanded justice never be perverted through partiality or bribery (Deut 16:18–20). Accusations required the testimony of two or three witnesses; and if someone provided false testimony, he ran the risk of receiving the penalty of the accused (Deut 19:15–21).

The three phases of the Jewish Trial included appearances before Annas, Caiaphas and the Sanhedrin Council (Figure 73).

First Jewish Phase, Before Annas (#154)

John 18:13–14, 19–23

From the Garden of Gethsemane, Jesus was whisked away to the home of Annas, who served as high priest from A.D. 6–15. Although he had not served in over 15 years, he was still recognized by the Jewish people as the high priest of God (John 18:13). The governor of Judea appointed the high priest annually, but Annas made sure he was succeeded only by his family members, including five of his sons and his son-in-law, Caiaphas.

Only John's Gospel records this important exchange between Annas and Jesus (John 18:13–14, 19–23). The interrogration took place late at night, possibly just after midnight. When questioned, Jesus confidently asserted he had done nothing wrong and had nothing to hide.

> "I have spoken openly to the world. I have always taught in synagogues and in the temple, where all Jews come together. I have said nothing in secret. Why do you ask me? Ask those who have heard me what I said to them; they know what I said" (John 18:20–21).

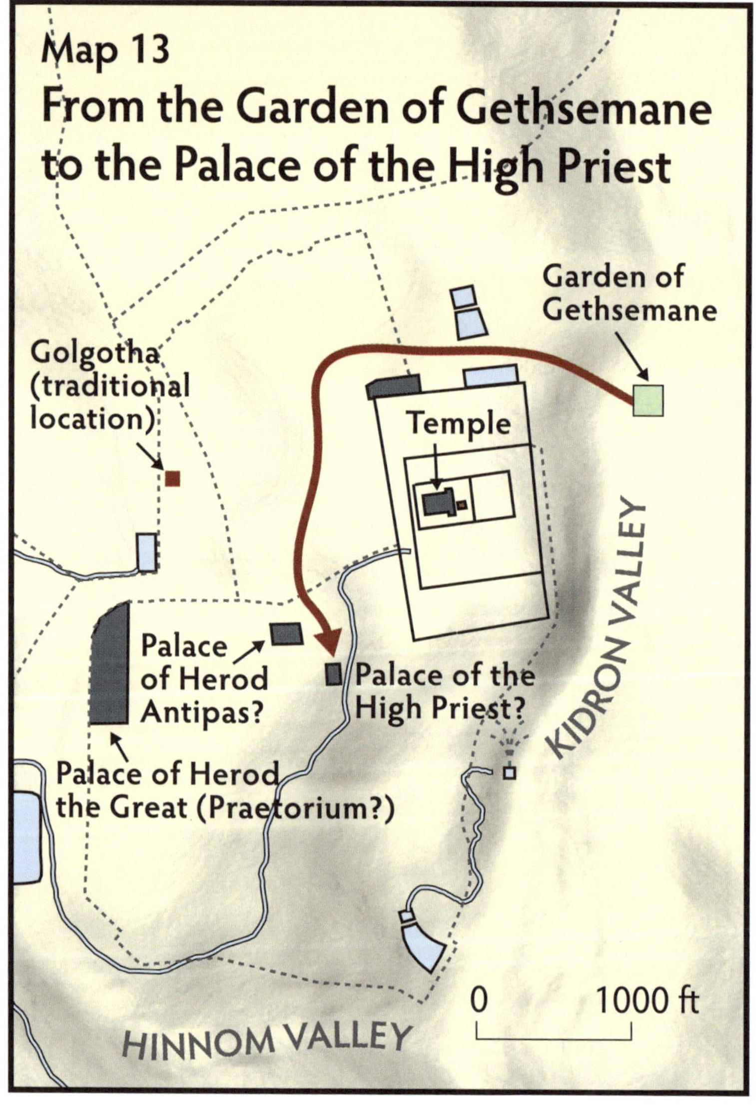

The Jewish Trial

Three Phases		Timeframe	Passages
Phase 1	Annas	midnight–1 A.M.	John 18:13–14, 19–24
Phase 2	Caiaphas; members of the Sanhedrin Council	1 A.M.–daybreak	Matt 26:57, 59–68; Mark 14:53, 55–65; Luke 22:54, 63–65; John 18:24
Phase 3	Sanhedrin Council	early in the morning	Matt 27:1–2; Mark 15:1; Luke 22:66–71

Figure 73.

An officer standing next to them hit Jesus in the face. "Is that how you answer the high priest?" he growled. Ironically, Jesus' accusers were the ones mishandling the proceedings because witnesses were supposed to be questioned before the defendant was. Annas was probably embarrassed by this implicit rebuke from Jesus. *"Ask those who heard me…"* Perhaps seeing Annas' response was what motivated the official to strike Jesus.

It would have been convenient if Jesus had perjured himself. Having failed to get something that could be used against Jesus, Annas sent him next door across the courtyard to the home of his son-in-law, Caiaphas.

Second Jewish Phase, Before Caiaphas (#155)

Matt 26:57, 59–68
Mark 14:53, 55–65
Luke 22:54a, 63–65
John 18:24

Jesus was taken to Annas first, giving Caiaphas time to gather members of the Sanhedrin Council to his home. Because these proceedings took place late at night, these men probably had to be awakened when they were summoned. They knew this was their best chance to eliminate Jesus. Matthew's reference to the "whole council" (Matt 26:59) likely referred to a quorum, a third of the Council, which would have been at least 23 members. Despite the late hour, the members of the Council made their way to Caiaphas' mansion overlooking the temple complex in Jerusalem's upper city.

Under the Law of Moses, the high priesthood was supposed to be a lifetime appointment, passed on from father to son. That changed under Herod the Great, however, who appointed and

This ornate limestone ossuary (bone box) was discovered in 1990 in Jerusalem. It is inscribed "Joseph, son of Caiaphas" and held the bones of a sixty-year-old male. It measures almost 15" high and 30" long.

deposed the high priest at will. After Herod's death in 4 B.C., Rome took over the appointment process. So as not to disrupt the peace, the religious leadership was typically kept within the current ruling families. As a result, Annas and his family dominated the high priesthood for decades, growing rich and powerful. They perceived Jesus to be a threat to their legacy. Now, the high priest had Jesus in his clutches.

Rather than being an example of piety and virtue, Annas and Caiaphas were greedy and corrupt (Figure 74). As the longest-serving high priest of the first century (A.D. 18–36), Caiaphas was a force to be reckoned with. Because Jesus was a threat to his hold on power, Caiaphas had to eliminate him.

A Contrast in High Priesthoods

Caiaphas	Jesus
Appointed high priest by Rome	The true high priest of God
Greedy and corrupt	Sinless and virtuous
Thought he was showing proper reverence to God	Jesus was the Son of God who was maligned and mistreated
Accused Jesus of blasphemy	Was, in fact, the Son of God
Was supposed to be impartial, but instead condemned Jesus	The true impartial judge who condemned Caiaphas

Figure 74.

Jesus had no legal counsel representing him when witnesses were sought to accuse him of blasphemy. The witnesses' testimony actually worked against Jesus' opponents, since many of the details in their testimony about Jesus were contradictory.

At one point, however, it seemed that the similar testimony of two witnesses would prove disastrous for Jesus. The men spoke about an earlier statement they remembered Jesus making right after the first cleansing of the temple at the beginning of his ministry (Matt 26:61; Mark 14:58; cf. John 2:19, #31).

> "Destroy this temple, and in three days I will raise it up" (John 2:19).

Like so many others who had also heard Jesus that day, these men misunderstood what he meant. He never said he was going to destroy the Herodian temple. Instead, Jesus was speaking about his own destruction by his death on the cross and his restoration at the subsequent resurrection. In the end, the testimony of these witnesses was to no avail. Because they could not agree on exactly what Jesus had said, their testimony had to be thrown out.

Then, Caiaphas took matters into his own hands. He demanded Jesus answer these accusations about destroying the temple. But instead of answering, Jesus said nothing at all.

The high priest would not give up. In desperation, he threw an explosive question at Jesus. "Are you the Christ, the Son of the Blessed One?" Jesus answered him.

> "I am, and you will see the Son of Man seated at the right hand of Power, and coming with the clouds of heaven" (Mark 14:62; cf. Matt 24:30; Dan 7:13).

Everyone understood what Jesus meant. He was applying the prophecy of Dan 7:13–14 to himself. In other words, he was claiming to be equal with God. He was also clearly indicating his future vindication since he would be seen riding with God on the clouds of heaven. Mere mortals did not ride on the clouds.

With his amazing answer, Jesus gave Caiaphas the ammunition he needed. Caiaphas tore his robes, even though the high priest was forbidden to do so (Lev 21:10), in feigned disbelief. "What further witnesses do we need?" he cried. "You have now heard his blasphemy" (Matt 26:65). Jesus was then declared to be deserving of death.

To further show their disdain for Jesus, the Sanhedrin Council members spit on him and hit him (Mark 14:65). They even made a game out of their mockery by covering his eyes and then demanding he identify his attacker. "Prophesy to us, you Christ!" they said, since Jesus claimed to be their long-awaited Messiah. The temple police joined in the cruel abuse.

The Suffering Servant

He was oppressed, and
he was afflicted, yet he
opened not his mouth;

Like a lamb that is led to the
slaughter, and like a sheep that
before its shearers is silent,
so he opened not his mouth.

—Isa 53:7

I gave my back to those who
strike, and my cheeks to those
who pull out the beard;

I hid not my face from
disgrace and spitting.

—Isa 50:6

This miscarriage of justice was orchestrated by Caiaphas. It had gone exactly according to his evil plan. Having conducted the proceedings at night, the religious leaders would need to wait until daylight hours to officially charge Jesus in the meeting place of the Sanhedrin Council. But the verdict had already been decided.

In the meantime, two of Jesus' apostles, Peter and John, witnessed these proceedings from afar. But Peter found himself having to deal with his own problems. He was recognized!

Matt 26:58, 69–75
Mark 14:54, 66–72
Luke 22:54b–62
John 18:15–18, 25–27

Peter's Denials (#156)

Peter's world had just been crushed. While in the Garden of Gethsemane, when Jesus needed him the most, he could not keep his eyes open and support Jesus (Matt 26:40–41, #152). And when he whipped out his sword, he had fully intended to protect Jesus or die trying. But he had failed at that, too.

At least he had been able to get inside the gate of the high priest's housing complex. Peter was in the courtyard in front of Caiaphas' house. Loud voices could be heard from the room above him where Jesus was being interrogated. Caiaphas and several members of the Sanhedrin Council were there, along with temple officers. Peter wanted to do something, but all he could do was wait helplessly. He knew it did not look good for Jesus.

Several servants and officers of the high priest had made a charcoal fire in the courtyard. Peter was sitting there, trying to keep himself warm in the cool night air, when a servant girl noticed him. She stared at him for a while and then said, "This man was with him!"

Peter had no idea how to react. And then, the words just came out of his mouth as naturally as anything. "No, I don't know him!"

No doubt, Peter was now feeling most uncomfortable. The temple guards made him nervous, but they did nothing to Peter. He got up and walked over to the covered entrance. Peter did not want to leave, but he might possibly need to make a quick getaway.

The same servant girl who first saw Peter began talking to another servant girl about him. "This man was with Jesus of Nazareth." Peter denied this second accusation, but this time with an oath. He swore by God that he did not even know Jesus, nor was he one of his disciples.

Peter certainly thought he might be in danger, especially with temple guards all around. So far, his denials had kept him safe. In the meantime, Jesus, who suffered violence from his accusers, bravely endured the terrible mistreatment he received.

Peter stayed and waited, wanting to see what would happen to Jesus. An hour passed by. People kept talking with Peter and looking at him. Finally, someone said, "Your accent gives you away. You're a Galilean! You must be one of his disciples." Someone else who was a relative of Malchus said, "Didn't I see you with him in the garden earlier tonight?"

A model of the palace of the high priest.

Peter really was scared now. He swore, calling down God's curses on himself if he was lying. "I don't know what you're talking about! I don't know the man!"

At that moment, Peter caught Jesus staring right back at him (Luke 22:61). Their eyes locked for what must have seemed like the longest time to Peter. And then, somewhere nearby, a rooster crowed.

The words of Jesus came back to him. *"Peter, the rooster will not crow until you deny three times that you know me."* Overwhelmed with shame and remorse, Peter fled—again.

The look on Jesus' face had broken his heart. How could Jesus ever forgive him? Peter cowered in the darkness and wept bitterly.

Matt 27:1
Mark 15:1a
Luke 22:66–71

Third Jewish Phase, Before the Sanhedrin (#157)

The Sanhedrin Council was the highest court in Israel and was housed in Herod's temple. The Council was comprised of 71 members, consisting of Pharisees and Sadducees. As high priest, Caiaphas served as its head.

The formal verdict during daylight hours gave the appearance of legality, which would help sway the public that their actions were conducted properly and the results were thus legitimate. But since the decision had been made hours before, the pronouncement of guilt was a ridiculous miscarriage of justice.

No one was called upon to stand in the defense of Jesus. Without any legal representation, Jesus was an easy target for the manipulations of Annas and Caiaphas. He was guilty in the eyes of the Council before the trial started. With the guilty verdict in hand, the religious leaders were now ready to hand over Jesus to the Pilate, the governor of Judea.

Matt 27:3–10
Acts 1:18–19

Judas Commits Suicide (#158)

When he saw that Jesus was condemned, Judas became remorseful. Jesus was going to be executed unless he somehow intervened. And so, Judas attempted to undo his betrayal by returning the money.

In his own way, Judas attested to Jesus' innocence. He told the priests, "I have sinned by betraying innocent blood" (Matt 27:4). His pleas fell on deaf ears, since the religious leaders had no interest in justice. They wanted Jesus dead.

Judas dramatically flung the bag of silver onto the floor of the temple. Feeling helpless and overwhelmed with guilt, he went out and hanged himself.

The priests picked up the money but refused to place it in the temple treasury, considering it to be blood money. Instead, they used it to buy a burial place for foreigners. They called the field *Akeldama* (pronounced a-KEL-dah-mah) which means, "Field of Blood" in Aramaic (Acts 1:19).

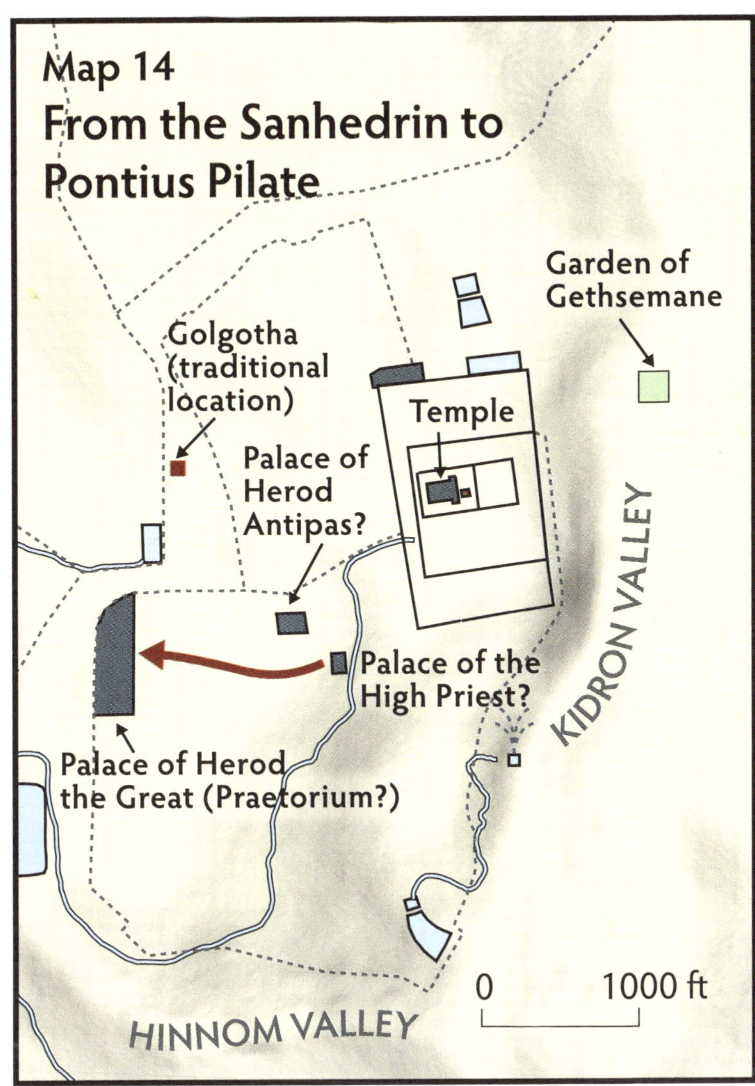

The Roman Trial (#159–161)

Matt 27:2, 11–26
Mark 15:1b–15
Luke 23:1–25
John 18:28–19:16a

Caiaphas wanted Jesus to die by crucifixion in part because it would inflict the greatest amount of pain. The Romans were especially proficient at crucifixion, but the only way to make this happen to Jesus was to have Pontius Pilate, the Roman governor of Judea, officially condemn Jesus, too. Caiaphas took Jesus before Pilate and charged Jesus with insubordination.

Like the Jewish Trial, the Roman Trial had three phases. Jesus made appearances before Pilate, then Herod Antipas, and finally back to Pilate for a final time (Figure 75).

Matt 27:2, 11–14
Mark 15:1b–5
Luke 23:1–5
John 18:28–38

First Roman Phase, Before Pilate (#159)

Pontius Pilate was the fifth Roman prefect, or governor, of Judea, serving at the behest of Caesar from A.D. 26–37. Notorious for his cruelty, Pilate had previously killed a group of rioting Galileans earlier in his career (see Luke 13:1, #109).

Pilate lived in the praetorium, a military fortress within the Herodian palace on the western part of Jerusalem. Having arrived at the governor's residence, these self-righteous Jewish leaders refused to enter because it would render them ceremonially unclean and thus unfit to partake of the Feast of Unleavened Bread.

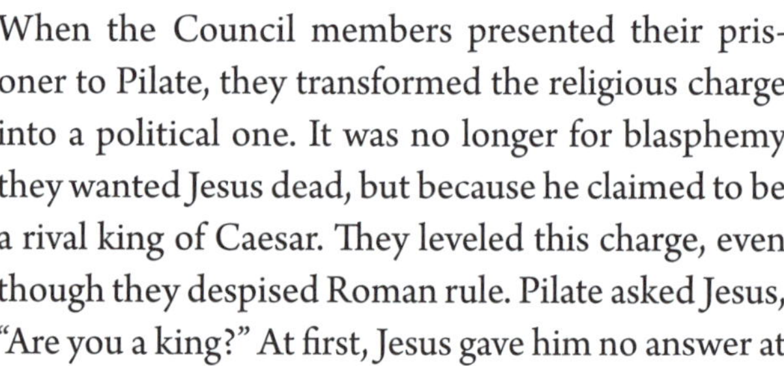

That they were in the process of murdering an innocent man seemed to be irrelevant. Their feigned piety required Pilate come out and meet them.

When the Council members presented their prisoner to Pilate, they transformed the religious charge into a political one. It was no longer for blasphemy they wanted Jesus dead, but because he claimed to be a rival king of Caesar. They leveled this charge, even though they despised Roman rule. Pilate asked Jesus, "Are you a king?" At first, Jesus gave him no answer at all, but eventually he responded.

> "You say that I am a king. For this purpose I was born and for this purpose I have come into the world—to bear witness to the truth. Everyone who is of the truth listens to my voice" (John 18:37).

Pilate gave a three-word response: "What is truth?" Ironically, the very embodiment of the truth was standing right in front of the Roman governor, but like the religious leaders, he failed to see Jesus for who he really was. Having voiced that rhetorical question, Pilate walked back to Jesus' accusers.

Pilate was a shrewd politician and perceived that the primary motivation for the religious leaders' hatred of Jesus was envy. To the dismay of the religious leaders, Pilate declared Jesus to be unworthy of their charge of insurrection (Luke 23:4; John 18:38).

Sensing the moment slipping from them, Caiaphas and his cohorts insisted Jesus must be punished.

> "He stirs up the people, teaching throughout all Judea, from Galilee even to this place" (Luke 23:5).

Upon the mention of "Galilee," Pilate grew excited. Because Jesus was from Galilee, he was under the jurisdiction of Herod Antipas, the ruler of Galilee. *How convenient*, Pilate must have thought, because Herod was currently only a 10-minute walk away, staying at his Jerusalem palace for the Passover (see Map 14 on page 111). Hoping to rid himself of his pesky problem, Pilate quickly made arrangements to send Jesus to Herod.

The Roman Trial

Three Phases		Timeframe	Passages
Phase 1	Pontius Pilate	early Friday morning	Matt 27:2, 11–14; Mark 15:2–5; Luke 23:1–5; John 18:28–38
Phase 2	Herod Antipas	early Friday morning	Luke 23:6–12
Phase 3	Pontius Pilate again	between 9 A.M. and noon	Matt 27:15–26; Mark 15:6–15; Luke 23:13–25; John 18:39–19:16

Figure 75.

Second Roman Phase, Before Herod Antipas (#160)

Luke 23:6–12

Throughout Jesus' Galilean ministry, Herod had heard about his miraculous activity and wanted to see Jesus perform one (Luke 9:9). Instead of cooperating with his request, Jesus refused to answer any of his questions and remained silent.

During Herod's interrogation of Jesus, the chief priests and scribes spewed vehement accusations against Jesus. Herod's own soldiers joined in the ruckus, ridiculing Jesus and mocking him by placing an elegant robe on him. Frustrated, Herod decided he could do nothing with Jesus and returned him to Pilate.

Prior to this event, Herod and Pilate had been at odds with each other, but would become friends (Luke 23:12) after their shared interrogation of Jesus.

Matt 27:15–26
Mark 15:6–15
Luke 23:13–25
John 18:39–19:16a

Third Roman Phase, Before Pilate Again (#161)

At Passover, it was traditional for the governor to release a prisoner. Still looking for a way out of this conflict with the religious leaders, Pilate asked them, "Do you want me to release 'the king of the Jews'?"

Known as the Pilate Inscription, a broken stone tablet discovered in Caesarea confirms the historical existence of Pontius Pilate, Prefect of Judea. The photo is a fascimile of this important artifact.

Caiaphas and his cohorts stirred up the crowds, inciting them to shout for the release of Barabbas instead.

> "Away with this man, and release to us Barabbas!" (Luke 23:18).

Unlike Jesus, Barabbas really was a violent insurrectionist against Roman rule. Earlier in the week, many people had lauded Jesus as the Messiah. But the guilty verdict from the Sanhedrin Council had swayed the crowds, persuading them to turn on Jesus and join in with the demand for his death.

By now, Pilate was convinced Jesus was innocent of the charges against him. In fact, his own wife strengthened his suspicions when she sent him an eerie message:

> "Have nothing to do with that righteous man, for I have suffered much because of him today in a dream" (Matt 27:19).

Romans typically took such dreams seriously as omens from the gods. But because Pilate's primary job was to keep the peace in Jerusalem, he had to find a way to appease the Jews. Otherwise, he would soon have a riot on his hands.

The Flogging

Pilate then made the decision to have Jesus flogged (John 19:1). Later, Jesus would be brutally scourged (Matt 27:26; Mark 15:15, #161). For now, Pilate hoped this lighter form of punishment would somehow satisfy the religious leaders.

In addition to flogging Jesus, the Roman soldiers twisted together a crown of thorns and placed it on his head. They hit him repeatedly in the face. No doubt, blood oozed profusely from his punctured skin. They mocked him by putting a purple robe on him and bowing down before him as they said, "Hail, king of the Jews!"

Pilate brought out Jesus. He looked pitiful as he wore this makeshift crown of thorns and bloodied robe. Upon seeing him, the religious leaders shouted, "Crucify him! Crucify him!" They were not satisfied by the flogging. Pilate's ploy had failed.

The Roman soldiers placed a "crown of thorns" on Jesus' head.

For the third time, Pilate declared Jesus' innocence (John 19:6; see also John 18:38; 19:4). With the tension growing insurmountable, the Jews pushed back hard.

> "We have a law, and according to that law he ought to die because he has made himself the Son of God" (John 19:7).

Pilate went to Jesus for further information. As a result of their previous conversation, coupled with his wife's mysterious dream, Pilate concluded that Jesus was otherworldly. "Where are you from?" he asked (John 19:9). But Jesus remained silent. Pilate grew impatient and demanded,

> "You will not speak to me? Do you not know that I have authority to release you and authority to crucify you?" (John 19:10).

Jesus at last responded to Pilate.

> "You would have no authority over me at all unless it had been given you from above. Therefore he who delivered me over to you has the greater sin" (John 19:11).

Pilate definitely understood he was on the verge of losing control of this volatile situation. Caiaphas and the religious leaders threatened him, suggesting that Jesus was a threat to Caesar.

> "If you release this man, you are not Caesar's friend. Everyone who makes himself a king opposes Caesar" (John 19:12).

Pilate was torn between the politically smart choice to give in and his belief that Jesus was no threat to Rome. With the growing fear of a riot, Pilate made his fateful decision. As he stood before the crowd, he had a basin of water brought out. He washed his hands as he said, "I am innocent of this man's blood; see to it yourselves" (Matt 27:24). Infamously, the crowd responded by saying, "His blood be on us and on our children!" (Matt 27:25). At that point, Pilate ordered the release of Barabbas and the scourging of Jesus.

The Scourging

Prior to his scourging, Jesus' hands would have been tied to a post. Two Roman soldiers on either side would have alternated whipping him with a whip that had pieces of bone or sharp metal at the ends of several short leather strings. His back and legs would be lacerated, tearing into the underlying skeletal muscles, producing ribbons of bleeding flesh. Many times, the victim of the scourging did not survive.

Conclusion

The condemnation of Jesus was a terrible miscarriage of justice orchestrated by Annas and Caiaphas. They and the Sanhedrin Council had originally intended to arrest Jesus after the Passover celebration (Matt 26:3–5, #140). But when one of his own apostles was willing to betray him, they adjusted their evil plans. It was too good an opportunity to pass up. If Jesus was arrested around midnight, then his trials took less than 12 hours.

Pontius Pilate and Herod Antipas certainly played their part in the death of Jesus (cf. Acts 4:27). But Caiaphas was primarily responsible. Jesus was referring to Caiaphas the high priest when he said to Pilate, "He who delivered me over to you has the greater sin."

Yet, Jesus laid down his life willingly. Ultimately, it was Jesus who was in control. The perfect, sinless Son of God was about to be sacrificed for the sins of mankind on a cross as part of God's master plan (cf. Acts 2:23).

WHAT DID YOU LEARN IN LESSON 13?

Match the key concept in the numbered list below with the letter of the phrase that best describes it. Answers appear upside-down at the bottom of the page.

Key Concepts

1. Caiaphas
2. Pilate
3. Judas
4. Sanhedrin Council
5. Annas
6. Malchus
7. Rooster
8. Praetorium
9. Barabbas
10. Crown of thorns
11. Akeldama
12. Scourging

Descriptions

A. The field where Judas was buried after his suicide. It literally means "field of blood."

B. Jesus' apostle who betrayed him for 30 pieces of silver.

C. The governor of Judea during the trial of Jesus.

D. The servant of the high priest. His ears was sliced off by Peter and immediately restored by Jesus during the arrest.

E. The animal Jesus predicted would be heard during Peter's denials.

F. The highest ruling body in the Jewish nation. It consisted of 71 members.

G. The acting high priest who played a vital part in securing Jesus' crucifixion from Rome.

H. A Jerusalem fortress that served as the headquarters for the Judean governor.

I. The insurrectionist and murderer who was released in place of Jesus.

J. A brutal beating that included two Roman soldiers alternating as they whipped their victim who was tied to a post.

K. The former high priest who presided over Jesus' first Jewish trial.

L. A cruel instrument of torture inflicted on Jesus' head by the Roman soldiers as they taunted him.

Answers

1G, 2C, 3B, 4F, 5K, 6D, 7E, 8H, 9I, 10L, 11A, 12J

WHAT DID YOU LEARN IN LESSON 13?

Do your best to answer the following questions. Some answers can be found in the text of Lesson 13, but not all of them. For others, you will be asked to look up passages in your Bible to find them.

Fill in the Blanks.

1. When he was arrested, Jesus asked, "Shall I not ________ the cup that the __________ has given me?" (John 18:11, #153).

2. Identify the three phases of Jesus' Jewish Trial.

   1. Before ______________________________ (#154)
   2. Before ______________________ and some members of the ______________________ Council (#155)
   3. Before the full ______________________ Council (#157)

3. Identify the three phases of Jesus' Roman Trial.

   1. Before ______________________________ (#159)
   2. Before Herod ______________________________ (#160)
   3. Before ______________________________ again (#161)

4. During the Roman Trial, whom did Pilate release instead of Jesus? ______________________ Why did he do this?

   ____

   ____

   ____

5. How did Judas identify Jesus to the Roman soldiers when they arrived to arrest Jesus? ______________________

   ____

   ____

   ____

6. During his interrogration of Jesus, why did Pilate send him to Herod Antipas? ____________________

____

____

____

____

Multiple Choice. Circle the correct answer.

1. Where was Jesus betrayed and arrested?
   A. In the temple.
   B. In the Garden of Gethsemane.
   C. At Lazarus' home.
   D. At the high priest's home.

2. During his arrest, what did Peter do to defend Jesus?
   A. He stood in front of Jesus, shielding him.
   B. He brandished a sword and attacked.
   C. He pretended to be Jesus so they wouldn't arrest him.
   D. He threatened to protest the arrest.

3. Why were Jesus' trials before the Jewish high priests such a mockery?
   A. They was conducted hurriedly at night.
   B. Jesus was never seriously considered innocent before proven guilty.
   C. The evidence presented was contradictory.
   D. All the above

4. Why did Pilate's wife want him to release Jesus?
   A. She was a disciple of Jesus.
   B. She told him they had a dinner appointment and he needed to hurry.
   C. She was afraid of being bullied by her friends if Jesus was crucified.
   D. She had a dream about Jesus that frightened her.

APPLICATION OF LESSON 13.

For Discussion.

1. The ossuary (burial bone box) of Caiaphas was discovered in 1990. We have physical evidence of Caiaphas' death and not Jesus' death. What thoughts do you have regarding this?

___

___

___

___

2. What do you think Pilate meant when he asked Jesus, "What is truth?" (John 18:38, #159)? ___

___

___

___

___

3. Pilate literally washed his hands of Jesus' crucifixion (Matt 27:24, #161; cf. Acts 3:13). Do you think God held Pilate guilty? Explain your answer. ___

___

___

___

4. Although he denied Jesus, Peter was given a second chance. How do you think his failures during Jesus' trials might have helped him later in life (see 1 Pet 3:15)? ___

___

___

___

___

LESSON 14

The Crucifixion (#162–168)

Matt 27:27–66
Mark 15:16–47
Luke 23:26–56
John 19:16b–42

Everything Jesus had done up to this point would culminate in his crucifixion. He "came into this world to save sinners" by dying for them (1 Tim 1:15). That moment had finally arrived.

Crucifixion (#162–166)

Matt 27:27–56
Mark 15:16–41
Luke 23:26–49
John 19:16b–30

Jesus' health was in shambles. He had not slept in 24 hours. Throughout the night, he had been repeatedly beaten. The brutal scourging would have caused considerable blood loss. His body was no doubt going into shock.

Mockery by the Roman Soldiers (#162)

Matt 27:27–30
Mark 15:16–19

After scourging Jesus, the Roman soldiers began to mock him. They clothed him with another robe ("scarlet robe," Matt 27:28; "purple cloak," Mark 15:17) and put the crown of thorns back on his head. To complete his kingly garb, they placed a reed in his hand to serve as his royal scepter. They repeatedly took it from him and beat him on the head, causing the long thorns of his "crown" to dig even deeper into his scalp and forehead. Blood would have flowed freely all over his face and into his eyes. "Hail, King of the Jews!" they said as they spit on him and hit him repeatedly on the head with the reed.

When the Roman soldiers were finished mocking him, they stripped him of the robe and placed his own clothes back on him. Very likely, tearing the robe from Jesus' back would have reopened his bloody wounds. Afterward, they led him away from the governor's palace to the crucifixion site.

Matt 27:31–34
Mark 15:20–23
Luke 23:26–33a
John 19:16b–17

The Journey to Golgotha (#163)

Jesus was crucified at Golgotha (pronounced GOL-guh-thuh). This word means "skull" in Aramaic. In Latin, it is called Calvary, which also means "skull." Although probably not very high, Golgotha is visible from just outside the city of Jerusalem (cf. Heb 13:12) and is often referred to as either Mount Calvary or the hill of Calvary.

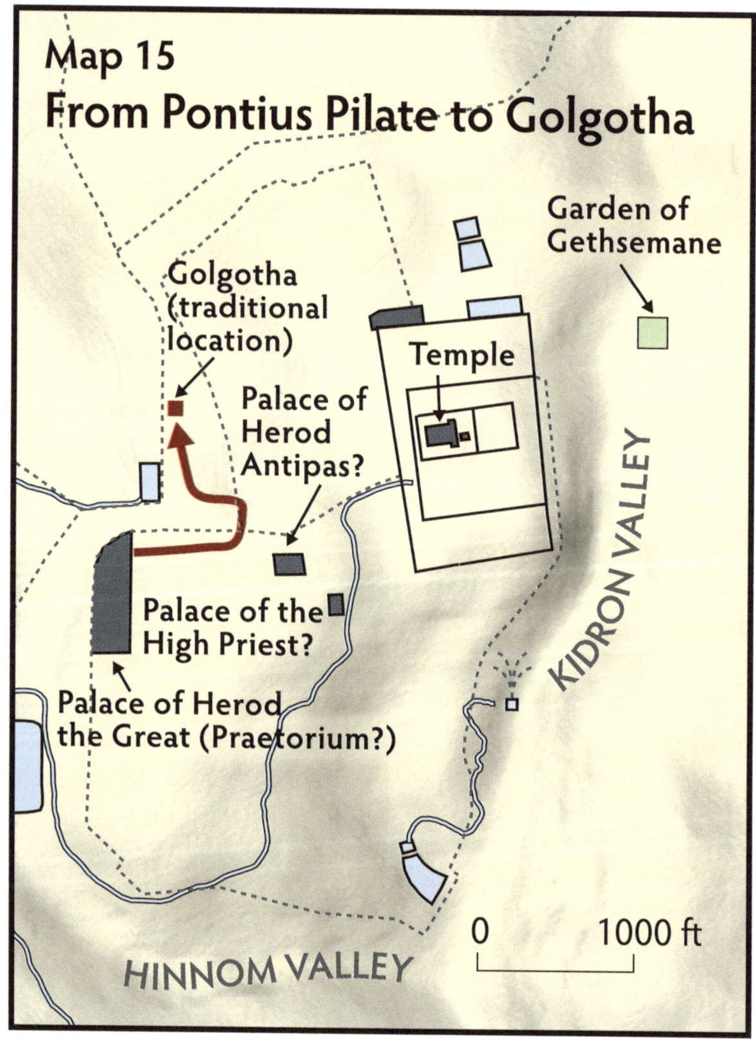

It was customary for the victim to carry his own cross from the scourging post to the crucifixion site. The crossbar (*patibulum* in Latin) was five to six feet long and weighed 75–125 lbs. Placed across the back of his neck and balanced along both shoulders, Jesus was expected to carry it about a third of a mile from the governor's palace to the top of the hill at Golgotha.

The Crossbar

The entire T-shaped cross would have weighed in excess of 300 lbs.

Jesus only carried the crossbar (which weighed 75–125 lbs.).

Jesus had become too weak to carry it all the way. A Jew by the name of Simon from Cyrene was compelled by the Romans to take the crossbar the remainder of the way.* How humiliating and terrifying it must have been for this man to have this extremely heavy wooden bar tied down to him with ropes as if he were a vile criminal.

Along the path to the cross, believers followed behind Jesus, wailing. Many of them were women. Jesus took a moment to speak to them, telling them not to mourn for him, but for themselves and the city of Jerusalem.

> "Daughters of Jerusalem, do not weep for me, but weep for yourselves and for your children" (Luke 23:28).

Even when facing his own death on the cross, Jesus took time to think of others. He spoke of the future destruction of Jerusalem, which would occur in A.D. 70. He warned his fellow Jews that, if the Romans would kill the perfect Son of God, it was unimaginable what they'd one day do to them and their city.

As the soldiers prepared to nail Jesus to the crossbar, they offered him wine mixed with myrrh (Mark 15:23; "gall," Matt 27:34), which was a mild narcotic and served as an anesthesia. When he tasted it, Jesus refused to drink it.

---

* Cyrene was a city on the north coast of Africa, near modern-day Benghazi. It had a large Jewish population in the first century A.D. Mark's account mentions Simon's two sons, Alexander and Rufus (Mark 15:21). Very likely, Simon became a disciple of Jesus and the first-century Christian community would have known this family. It is possible Simon's son was the "Rufus" mentioned in Rom 16:13, although there is no way to know this with certainty.

Matt 27:35–44
Mark 15:24–32
Luke 23:33b–43
John 19:18–27

First Three Hours of Crucifixion (#164)

Atop Mount Calvary, there would have been an upright wooden stipe that stood about 6–8 feet tall jutting from the ground. It was ready to receive the crossbar and thus complete the T-shaped cross. The victim would be thrown to the ground on his back. At that point, his arms would have been nailed to the crossbar. Four Roman soldiers expertly carried out Jesus' crucifixion (cf. John 19:23).

The Roman soldiers were experts at inflicting the most horrific amount of pain possible.

Jesus Nailed to the Cross

The nails were tapered iron spikes approximately five to seven inches long. English translations indicate that the nails went through Jesus' "hands" (cf. Luke 24:40, #178), but this word can mean "wrists." (If the nails had gone through his hands, his weight would have caused the nails to tear through his knuckles while he hung on the cross.) The nails hammered through the wrists would have crushed and severed the median nerve, causing paralysis in his hands. The pain would have been excruciating.

After his arms were nailed to the crossbar, the victim would have been lifted up onto the wooden stipe already at the crucifixion site. The feet were then nailed to the stipe. Although no bones would have been broken in either the wrists or the feet (cf. John 19:36, #167a), the nerve damage would have sent shock waves of pain throughout the victim's body.

Despite his agony, Jesus had the presence of mind to look down on the perpetrators of his crucifixion and forgive them.

> "Father, forgive them, for they know not what they do" (Luke 23:34).

Instead of reacting with bitterness or hatred, the perfect Son of God practiced what he had preached by loving his enemies (cf. Matt 5:44). He did all this while hanging on the cross.

The Time of the Crucifixion

According to Mark's account, Jesus was crucified "the third hour" (Mark 15:25). But John's account says it was "the sixth hour" when Pilate handed over Jesus to be crucified (John 19:14).

Corresponding to our system of hours and minutes, the crucifixion occurred either at 9 A.M. ("third hour") or noon ("sixth hour").

The first-century world expressed time in terms of "watches" (Figure 76). They used four three-hour intervals to divide the daylight hours and four corresponding intervals to divide the nighttime hours (cf. Mark 6:48; 13:35). Mark rounds down to the third hour (9 A.M.) while John seems to be rounding up to the sixth (noon).

Ancient Jewish Time System by Watches

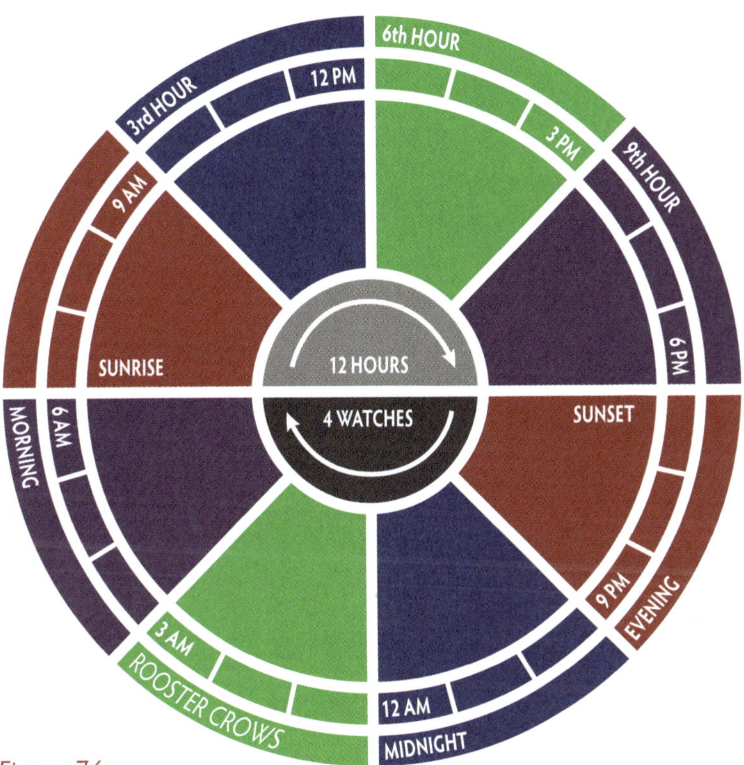

Figure 76.

Why the difference? The Passover lamb was traditionally slain at the sixth hour (i.e., noon). Thousands of lambs were slaughtered at the temple the day before, on Thursday. Having announced at the beginning of his Gospel that Jesus was "the Lamb of God" (John 1:29, #27), John made a clear connection between the two and likely rounded up to the "sixth hour."

The Inscription on the Cross

A sign (*titulus* in Latin) detailing the charges was placed above the victim's head. The words at the top of Jesus' cross were "Jesus of Nazareth, the King of the Jews" (John 19:19). The inscription was written in three languages—Greek, Latin, and Aramaic—so everyone would be able to understand it.

The chief priests were upset by the wording and argued with Pilate that the charge should instead more clearly indicate Jesus only claimed to be a king. Pilate responded tersely, "What I have written, I have written" (John 19:22).

Groups of People Present at the Crucifixion

Many different people were at Golgotha during Jesus' crucifixion (Figure 77), including the four Roman soldiers who carried out Jesus' execution. In derision of their crucified victim, they divided Jesus' clothes among themselves. These items would have included his sandals, a belt, and a tunic. Because his tunic was "seamless, woven in one piece from top to bottom" (John 19:23), they instead cast lots for it.

People Present at the Crucifixion

Groups	Citations
Four Roman soldiers who executed him	John 19:23
Unnamed bystanders	Matt 27:47; Mark 15:29–30; Luke 23:48
Chief priests and scribes	Mark 15:31–32
Two criminals	Matt 27:38
Jesus' mother, Mary	John 19:25
Several disciples, including John ("the disciple whom Jesus loved")	Luke 23:49; John 19:25–27
Roman centurion	Mark 15:39; Luke 23:47

Figure 77.

Several unnamed bystanders derided Jesus while he hung on the cross. The chief priests and scribes were also present to gloat over Jesus' humiliation. As they watched Jesus writhe in pain and agony, they continued to ridicule him with sarcastic taunts.

> "Let the Christ, the King of Israel, come down now from the cross that we may see and believe" (Mark 15:32).

Jesus was not the only one crucified that day on Golgotha. Two criminals were executed alongside him. One was hung on his right and the other on his left. At first, both of these men joined in deriding Jesus (Matt 27:44). Then, one of them rebuked the other and proceeded to confess faith in Jesus, calling him "Lord." The man even asked Jesus to do something for him:

> "Jesus, remember me when you come into your kingdom" (Luke 23:42).

While he hung on a cross alongside Jesus, this "thief on the cross" demonstrated a strong belief that somehow Jesus' death on the cross would result in ultimate triumph. Jesus responded to his confession with words of forgiveness and hope:

> "Truly I say to you, today you will be with me in paradise" (Luke 23:43).

Also present at the cross were those who loved Jesus dearly, including his own mother, Mary (John 19:23). No doubt, at that moment, she felt the truth of Simeon's prophecy spoken to her over 30 years before when Jesus was presented in the Temple shortly after his birth: "a sword will pierce through your own soul also" (Luke 2:35, #13). Several other women were there, too, supporting her in this dark moment of her life (John 19:25). The only male disciple mentioned was "the disciple whom Jesus loved," John. As he stood next to Jesus' mother, Jesus asked John to take care of Mary.

> "Woman, behold your son!"... "Behold, your mother!" (John 19:26).

Despite his own terrible agony, Jesus had the presence of mind to provide for his mother.

Last Three Hours of the Crucifixion (#165)

Matt 27:45–50
Mark 15:33–37
Luke 23:44–45a, 46
John 19:28–30

The most important event in all of history happened on a lonely hill just outside the city of Jerusalem. The battle for the redemption of humanity seemed to be slipping away. Seemingly, all Jesus could do was look down from the cross as his enemies derided him and his friends looked on helplessly.

As the second half of this monumental event began, an ominous darkness permeated the sky. It was a miraculous event lasting three hours (Mark 15:33). When the sun should have been at its brightest, darkness covered the land.

At this point, Jesus uttered the fourth of seven sayings from the cross (Figure 78). He cried out loudly:

> "My God, my God, why have you forsaken me?" (Matt 27:46).

Seven Sayings of Jesus from the Cross

Saying	Citation
1. "Father, forgive them, for they know not what they do."	Luke 23:34
2. "Truly, I say to you, today you will be with me in paradise."	Luke 23:43
3. "Woman, behold, your son!… Behold, your mother!"	John 19:26–27
4. "Eli, Eli, lema sabachthani?" which means, "My God, my God, why have you forsaken me?"	Matt 27:46; Mark 15:34
5. "I thirst."	John 19:28
6. "It is finished!"	John 19:30
7. "Father, into your hands I commit my spirit!"	Luke 23:46

Figure 78.

He spoke these words in his native Aramaic, causing some people to be confused when they heard it.

> And about the ninth hour Jesus cried out with a loud voice, saying, "Eli, Eli, lema sabachthani?" that is, "My God, my God, why have you forsaken me?" And some of the bystanders, hearing it, said, "This man is calling Elijah" (Matt 27:46–47).

When they heard the word "Eli," some seemingly thought he was calling for the Old Testament prophet, Elijah. Someone turned this into another taunt saying, "Let's see if Elijah will come and save him!" But that's not what Jesus was trying to say. Rather,

Jesus was quoting the opening words of Ps 22: "My God, my God, why have you forsaken me?"

Many believe that this pitiful cry from Jesus supports the idea that God turned his back on Jesus (cf. 2 Cor 5:21). What must not be overlooked is that Psalm 22 is actually a victory song in which David expresses his utmost confidence in God to deliver him.

> For he has not despised or abhorred
> the affliction of the afflicted,
> and he has not hidden his face from him,
> but has heard, when he cried to him (Ps 22:24).

> "For our sake he made him to be sin who knew no sin, so that in him we might become the righteousness of God.
> —2 Cor 5:21"

Nearing the end of his life, Jesus said, "I thirst" (John 19:28). His throat was quite parched, and Jesus wanted to quench his thirst before he uttered his final victory cry.

Remarkably, the Roman soldiers permitted some of their wine vinegar to be given to him. The drink was lifted up to Jesus' mouth by a sponge at the end of a hyssop branch. It would have needed only to be a couple of feet long to reach him. Having received this little bit of refreshment, Jesus was now ready to utter his last words: "It is finished!" (John 19:30).

Jesus said these words of victory because he knew he was on the cusp of dying for the sins of humanity. The work of redemption was just about to be accomplished. He had lived a sinless and perfect life. He had drunk the cup the Father gave him to drink. It was finished!

> Lifted up was he to die;
> "It is finished!" was his cry. . . .
> Hallelujah! What a Savior!*

Just before his spirit left his body, Jesus said, "Father, into your hands I commit my spirit!" (Luke 23:46). This final cry of victory took all the effort he had left. His body went limp as it hung on the cross of Calvary. From that moment on, nothing would ever be the same.

* "What a Savior," words and music by Philip P. Bliss (1838–1876).

Matt 27:51–56
Mark 15:38–41
Luke 23:45b, 47–49

Witnesses of Jesus' Death (#166)

At the moment when Jesus died, three amazing events occurred.

1. The curtain of the temple was torn in half, from the top and to the bottom.
2. An earthquake rocked the surrounding area, causing rocks to break and split apart.

Golgotha and the Temple Mount

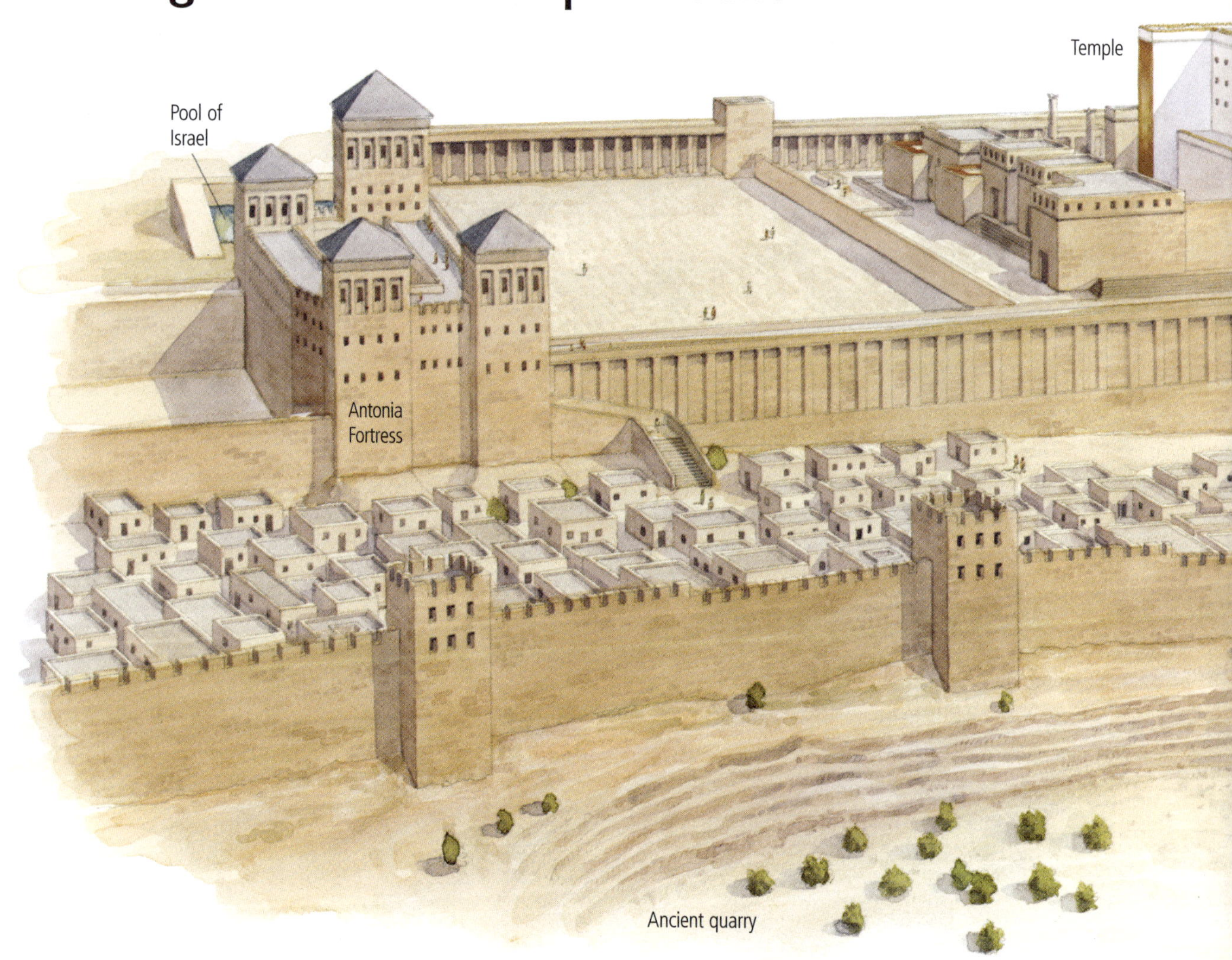

3. Various tombs were broken open in the area. (Later, when Jesus was raised from the dead, people who were also dead will emerged from these tombs and entered the city of Jerusalem.)

The Jewish temple had two veils associated with it. Inside, a large veil separated the two innermost rooms where the priests performed the daily sacrifices. The Holy Place was separated from the Most Holy Place by this veil. Only the high priest was allowed

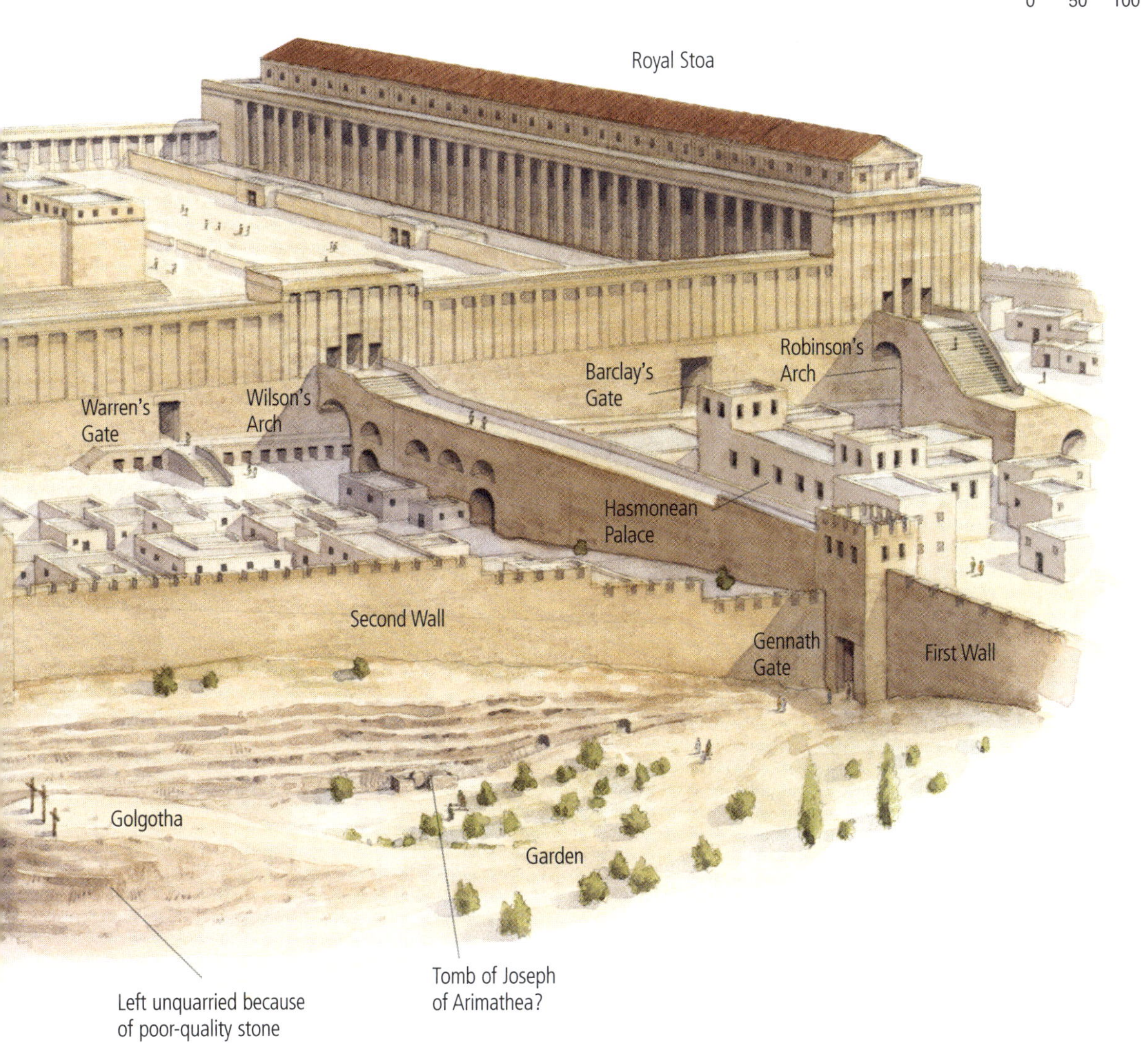

"Torn Open"

And when he came up out of the water, immediately he saw the heavens being **torn** open.

—Mark 1:10

And the curtain of the temple was **torn** in two, from top to bottom.

—Mark 15:38

The outside veil of the Temple depicted the sky.

According to Mark's Gospel, Jesus' ministry begins and ends with the "heavens" being torn open.

to enter into this inner sanctum and approach God. And, he only could do that once a year, on the Day of Atonement (Ex 30:10). The destruction of this veil was symbolic, representing the removal of the barrier that separated humanity from God. Jesus' sacrificial death permanently opened the way into the presence of God (cf. Heb 4:16; 10:19).

It may have been the outside veil that suddenly ripped apart. Measuring 80 feet high, it was large enough to be seen from Golgotha (see pages 130–131). The curtain, which was beautifully embroidered with blue, scarlet and purple linens, depicted the starry sky (*J.W.*, 5.5.4 #212–14). At the moment Jesus died, it would have been ripped apart from top to bottom.

Standing in front of Jesus' cross was a Roman centurion who had overseen the entire crucifixion. When he heard Jesus say his final words and witnessed these violent events, the centurion responded by saying, "Truly this man was the Son of God!" (Mark 15:39). He even praised God, adding, "Certainly this man was innocent!" (Luke 23:47). He was amazed at the sudden and dramatic events that took place right after Jesus died.

With Jesus dead and the sun setting soon, the crowds began to disperse and return home. Overwhelmed with grief (Luke 23:48), the disciples descended the hill called Calvary.

Matt 27:57–66
Mark 15:42–47
Luke 23:50–56
John 19:31–42

Burial (#167–168)

Normally, a crucifixion victim would be left on the cross for days. But the Sabbath was only a few short hours away. Because the next day was also the start of the Feast of Unleavened Bread, it was called a "high day" (John 19:31). And so, for religious reasons, the Jews did not want the bodies left out past sunset.

Matt 27:57–58
Mark 15:42–45
Luke 23:50–52
John 19:31–38

Joseph Asks for Jesus' Body (#167a)

A rich and influential Jew by the name of Joseph of Arimathea wanted to bury Jesus in his own private tomb. As a member of the Sanhedrin Council (Matt 27:57; Mark 15:43), Joseph was risking his own reputation by revealing himself as a sympathizer of the Jesus movement. Being a devout Jew, he also appreciated the urgency of the moment. The sun was working its way toward the west and would set around 6 P.M. This would mark the start of the Sabbath.

The veil inside the temple separated the holy place from the most holy place.

Joseph went to Pilate and asked for Jesus' body. The governor was taken aback by this request, because he had no idea Jesus was already dead (Mark 15:44). Upon confirmation of Jesus' death, Pilate granted the body to be taken down and given to Joseph.

Jesus' Death Is Confirmed

To expedite the death of a crucifixion victim, the Romans would sometimes perform a procedure called crucifracture. Using a heavy club or iron mallet, they would break the legs of the crucified victims below the knees. This final act of cruelty would render the criminal unable to hold himself up to breathe, leading to asphyxiation within minutes. Because Jesus was dead, the Romans did not break his legs. The two criminals were still alive, however, and they suffered this terrible fate (John 19:32).

By not breaking Jesus' legs, the Romans unwittingly helped to fulfill Old Testament prophecy (see Figure 79). According to the Law of Moses, the Passover lamb was supposed to be perfect and without blemish. The Israelites were specifically commanded to roast it whole and not to break any of its bones (Ex 12:46). Jesus, as "the Lamb of God who takes away the sin of the world" (John 1:29, #81), was without blemish. With none of his bones broken, Jesus became the true Lamb of God by his sacrifice for sin.

Jesus' Side Is Pierced

To confirm Jesus' death, one of the soldiers took a spear and pierced his side, probably penetrating his heart. John says "blood and water" came out of the wound (John 19:34), likely referring to the pericardial fluid that surrounded the heart. This final act confirmed unequivocally that Jesus, after just a few hours on the cross, was dead.

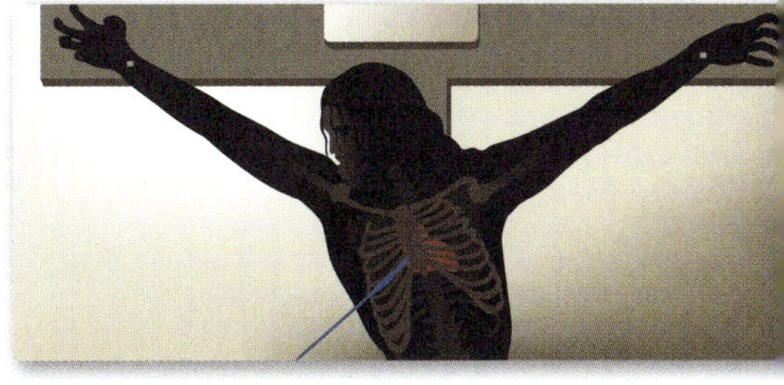

Matt 27:59–60
Mark 15:46
Luke 23:53–54
John 19:39–42

Jesus Is Buried (#167b)

Joseph of Arimathea was helped by his fellow Council member, Nicodemus, who provided a generous amount of spices (John 19:39). Following traditional Jewish burial customs, they wrapped the body of Jesus in linen cloths, layering them with a pasty mixture of aloes and myrrh. The aromatic spices would help to mask the smell of the decaying body. It is important to note that, while obviously in the minority, at least two members of the Sanhedrin were supporters of Jesus.

Old Testament Echoes in the Crucifixion of Jesus

Old Testament Quotation	OT Citation	NT Citation
"You shall not break any of its [the Passover lamb's] bones."	Ex 12:46	John 19:36
My God, my God, why have you forsaken me?	Ps 22:1	Matt 27:46; Mark 15:34
They have pierced my hands and feet.	Ps 22:16	Luke 23:33; cf. 24:40; John 20:25
They divide my garments among them, and for my clothing they cast lots.	Ps 22:18	John 19:24
"Father, into your hands I commit my spirit!"	Ps 31:5	Luke 23:46
He keeps all his bones; not one of them is broken.	Ps 34:20	Luke 23:34
For my thirst they gave me sour wine to drink.	Ps 69:21	Matt 27:48; Luke 23:36; John 19:29
I offered my back to those who beat me . . . I did not hide my face from mockery and spitting.	Isa 50:6	Matt 26:67; 27:26
And they made his grave with the wicked and with a rich man in his death.	Isa 53:9	Matt 27:57, 60
When they look on me, on him whom they have pierced, they shall mourn for him . . .	Zech 12:10	John 19:37

Figure 79.

Matt 27:61–66
Mark 15:47
Luke 23:55–56

The Women Watch and the Soldiers Guard (#168)

Several devout women who were disciples of Jesus had witnessed his body being taken down from the cross (Mark 15:40). They followed the procession to Joseph's private cemetery and watched the burial (Mark 15:47). These women were some of Jesus' most loyal disciples, including Mary Magdalene and Mary the mother of Joses.

The Women Plan to Return

Despite the efforts of Joseph and Nicodemus, these women were determined to return on Sunday after the Sabbath to lovingly and more properly prepare Jesus' body for burial. In the meantime, all they could do was go home and grieve. As they observed the Passover in their respective homes, they also prepared their own burial ointments and spices. They were intent on returning with them to the tomb early Sunday morning.

The Tomb Is Secured and Guarded

Being wealthy, Joseph of Arimathea had a large circular stone that covered the entrance of his family's tomb. The enemies of Jesus decided to use this stone to their advantage. On the Sabbath, the chief priests and the Pharisees approached Pilate and suggested the stone be rolled and sealed. In addition, they wanted soldiers to stand guard for three days.

The religious leaders remembered what Jesus' own disciples had seemingly forgotten. Jesus had repeatedly claimed that, when he was killed, he would rise from the dead after three days (cf. Matt 12:38–40). Pilate granted them permission, telling them to "make it as secure as you can" (Matt 27:65).

Conclusion

Even though they had been told repeatedly by Jesus to anticipate his subsequent resurrection, none of his followers seemed to remember. Their grief was simply too strong and overwhelming. In their minds, it was over. Jesus, whom everyone hoped was going to redeem Israel, went up against the chief priests and rulers—and lost his life in the process. This amazing man, despite his miracles and beautiful words, had been killed cruelly and violently. And his death happened so suddenly. The fervor of hope that had swept the nation was dramatically and crushingly brought to an end.

The Sabbath day started the Feast of Unleavened Bread. Normally, this holiday brought great joy to the Jewish people. This year, the hearts of Jesus' disciples were numb with disbelief.

But Sunday was coming…

WHAT DID YOU LEARN IN LESSON 14?

Match the key concept in the numbered list below with the letter of the phrase that best describes it. Answers appear upside-down at the bottom of the page.

Key Concepts

1. Golgotha
2. Joseph of Arimathea
3. Spear
4. Crossbar
5. Simon of Cyrene
6. Titulus
7. Iron spikes
8. Crucifracture
9. Lots
10. Veil
11. Seal
12. Crucifixion

Descriptions

A. The rich member of the Sanhedrin Council who asked Pilate for Jesus' body in order to bury it.

B. What the Roman soldiers used to nail Jesus to the cross. They would have measured approximately 5–7 inches long.

C. A Jewish man who was compelled to carry Jesus' crossbar to the crucifixion site.

D. What the four Roman soldiers cast to determine who would win Jesus' seamless robe as a prize.

E. The punishment inflicted on Jesus in order to kill him.

F. The Roman practice of breaking the legs of a crucifixion victim.

G. The very large and ornate tapestry that separated the Holy Place from the Most Holy Place inside the temple.

H. The hill outside Jerusalem where Jesus was crucified. It literally means "the skull" and is also called Calvary in Latin.

I. What a Roman soldier used to pierce Jesus' side and confirm his death on the cross.

J. The part of the cross a victim's hands were nailed to. It measured 5–6 feet long and weighed 75–125 lbs.

K. What was placed on the tomb of Jesus in order to secure it.

L. The sign Pilate placed on top of Jesus' cross with the charges written on it in three languages.

Answers

1H, 2A, 3I, 4J, 5C, 6L, 7B, 8F, 9D, 10G, 11K, 12E

WHAT DID YOU LEARN IN LESSON 14?

Do your best to answer the following questions. Some answers can be found in the text of Lesson 14, but not all of them. For others, you will be asked to look up passages in your Bible to find them.

Fill in the Blanks.

1. Why was Jesus offered wine mixed with myrrh during his crucifixion? ______________________________

____

____

2. As Jesus carried his crossbar to the crucifixion site, he told several women to ctop crying for him and cry for whom instead (Luke 23:28, #163)? ______________________________

____

Why did he tell them this? ______________________________

____

____

3. During Jesus' crucifixion, darkness was "over the whole land" from "the sixth hour" until "the ninth hour" (Luke 23:44, #164). What time of day was this? ______________________________

____

____

4. Explain why Joseph of Arimathea and Nicodemus hurriedly buried Jesus shortly after his death (see John 19:31).

____

____

____

____

5. What miraculous events took place when Jesus died on the cross (#166)?

a. ______________________________

b. ______________________________

c. ______________________________

5. Explain why it was important for Jesus' body to not have any broken bones when he was crucified. ______________________________

____

____

____

Multiple Choice. Circle the correct answer.

1. What is the name of the hill on which Jesus was crucified?
   A. Golgotha.
   B. Calvary.
   C. The Place of a Skull.
   D. All the above.

2. While hanging on the cross, what did Jesus say to the people below who were ridiculing him (Luke 23:34).
   A. "God will strike you dead!"
   B. "I will be raised from the dead and get even with you!"
   C. "Father, send angels to destroy them."
   D. "Father, forgive them."

3. What did the sign Pilate place above Jesus' cross say?
   A. "This will happen to you if you rebel against Rome."
   B. "Jesus of Nazareth, the King of the Jews."
   C. "Jesus claimed to be the Son of God."
   D. "Jesus the traitor of Rome."

APPLICATION OF LESSON 14.

For Discussion.

1. The Law of Moses says that someone is cursed if they are hanged on a tree (Deut 21:23; Gal 3:13). Do you think that Caiaphas wanted Jesus to die on the cross because he thought this would make Jesus be cursed of God? ____________

   ____

   ____

   ____

2. Jesus told one of the two criminals crucified with him, "Truly I say to you, today you will be with me in paradise" (Luke 23:43). Explain what you think this implies about where Jesus' spirit went after he died. ____________

   ____

   ____

   ____

3. After Jesus died, a Roman centurion standing nearby said, "Truly this was the Son of God!" (Matt 27:54; Mark 15:39, #166). Why did he say this? ____________

   ____

   ____

4. While on the cross, Jesus yelled out, "My God, my God, why have you forsaken me?" Explain why you think Jesus said these words (see Ps 22:1; Matt 27:46). ____________

   ____

   ____

   ____

   ____

LESSON 15

The Resurrection (#169–184)

Matt 28
Mark 16
Luke 24
John 20–21
1 Cor 15:5–7; Acts 1:3–12

When Jesus raised Lazarus of Bethany to life (John 11:17, #118), Annas and Caiaphas knew many people in town for the Passover would hear about it, since Bethany was only a couple miles from Jerusalem. This close proximity had motivated the religious leaders to move against Jesus quickly.

Originally, they did not want to act against Jesus during the Passover celebration (Matt 26:5, #140). How fortunate it was when Judas, one of Jesus' own apostles, had betrayed him, compelling the high priests to change their tactics. They could not have planned it any better. Because the crucifixion of Jesus took place during Passover, a lot more people saw the imposter's demise on the cross and now knew for sure he was a phony Messiah.

The charge of blasphemy had worked to discredit Jesus and sway the crowds against him. And, the charge of insurrection worked to persuade the Roman governor, Pilate.

Jesus was dead. The threat was over!

Matt 28:1–8
Mark 16:1–8
Luke 24:1–12
John 20:1–10

The Empty Tomb (#169–172)

The resurrection of Jesus is the cornerstone of our faith. Without it, Christianity crumbles, as the Apostle Paul says in his great discourse on the resurrection: "If Christ has not been raised, your faith is futile and you are still in your sins" (1 Cor 15:17). He then added, "But in fact Christ has been raised from the dead" (v. 20).

How Long Was Jesus in the Tomb?

He was buried on Friday afternoon around 6 P.M.

He rose from the dead on Sunday morning around 6 A.M.

Jesus spent three days in the tomb (Friday–Sunday), but was only in it about 36 hours total.

The Gospels go to great lengths to provide us with several vivid eyewitness accounts of Jesus' resurrection. We feel the heart-wrenching angst of the women who first discovered the empty tomb. We lose ourselves in the thick cloud of doubt and despair that hung over the weak and unbelieving disciples. At first, on the Sunday morning after his crucifixion, the disciples would grapple with the discovery of an empty tomb without a body.

And then, quite suddenly, we come face-to-face with the triumphant Jesus who has overcome death. His body bore the marks of his ordeal, but he had risen from the dead and paved the way for all of us to follow him. Ever in control, Jesus repeatedly presented himself to his disciples and showed them that fear and doubt had given way to faith and hope.

As Jesus patiently and lovingly tried to build the faith of his followers, the Gospel accounts also do the same for us.

Matt 28:1–8
Mark 16:1–8
Luke 24:1–8
John 20:1

The Women at the Empty Tomb (#169–171)

Early Sunday morning, while it was still dark, the women were approaching the cemetery, just like they had planned to do the Friday before. As they drew closer, they started wondering about how they would gain entrance. There was a huge circular stone blocking the tomb. How were they going to get it moved?

Not long before the women arrived at the tomb, an earthquake occurred. It was caused by a mighty angel who descended suddenly from the sky. The angel then single-handedly rolled the large stone out of the way and triumphantly sat on top of it.

The soldiers guarding the tomb were terrified.

Once the women were there, they saw the stone had been rolled away. The women were even more startled when they saw two young men dressed in white robes *inside* the tomb. They were angels. One of the two had just opened the tomb. They were waiting patiently for the women to arrive.

One of the angels spoke to the women. "You seek Jesus who was crucified," he told them. And then, what he said next upset them terribly. "Why do you seek the living among the dead?" (Luke 24:5). "He has risen; he is not here. See the place where they laid him" (Mark 15:6).

These women had come to anoint the body of Jesus. And now, they couldn't, because his body was missing. When they heard the angel's words, a mixture of fear and joy gripped their hearts.

The angel told them to go and tell Jesus' disciples that Jesus had been raised from the dead. Interestingly, the angel singled out Peter as someone who especially needed to hear this message. The last time he had seen Jesus alive, Peter was in the process of denying him (#156, pages 108–109).

The first eyewitnesses of the empty tomb were women, not the men (Figure 80). This was significant because, in the ancient world, the testimony of women was given a low status. Not surprisingly, when they later told the men about the morning's events, they were not taken seriously.

The Women at the Tomb

Name	Citation
Mary Magdalene	Matt 28:1; Mark 16:1; Luke 24:10; John 20:1
Mary, the mother of James the younger	Mark 16:1; Luke 24:10
Salome	Mark 16:1
Joanna	Luke 24:10; cf. Luke 8:3
"Other women"	Luke 24:10

Figure 80.

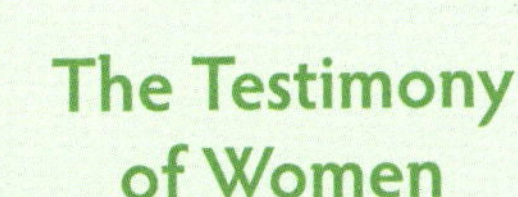

The Testimony of Women

> From women let no evidence be accepted, because of the levity and temerity of their sex.
>
> —*Ant.*, 4.219

Luke 24:9–12
John 20:2–10

Peter and John at the Empty Tomb (#172)

Dejected and despondent over Jesus' death, the disciples met at a secret location in Jerusalem (cf. John 20:19, #177; Luke 24:33, #178). They considered the women's tale about the morning's events simply too incredible to be true. Wallowing in their disappointment, they struggled to take seriously the women's report.

- Why was the stone rolled away?
- Who were these "men in dazzling clothing" and what were they doing at the tomb?
- Why were they saying Jesus was alive?

It all seemed too strange and unbelievable. They knew Jesus was dead, and nothing was going to change that.

The most confusing detail of all was what the women said they *didn't* see. Jesus' body was no longer where it was supposed to be. According to them, the body was gone!

Several of the men started toward the tomb after deciding to investigate for themselves (cf. Luke 24:24, #176). Among them were Peter and John ("the other disciple" in John 20:2–4) who hurriedly ran to it. John got there first, but waited until Peter arrived before going in. While standing at the entrance and stooping in to look, John could see the grave cloths lying where the body should have been.

When he made it to the tomb, Peter immediately entered. John followed him, and together they took a closer look at the grave cloths. There was no body inside them. And they also noticed something else: The head scarf was carefully rolled up and placed where the head had been resting.

Peter stood there, wondering what had happened. Obviously, the body was gone, but why would someone leave the grave cloths behind? It didn't make any sense.

John, after taking in the whole scene, began to put the pieces together. Doubt gave way to faith as he came to accept that maybe—just maybe—the women were right. Could Jesus really be alive?

Peter and John ("the other disciple") saw the same scene the women had seen and reported. After examining the evidence, only John's faith began percolating.

> Then the other disciple, who had reached the tomb first [John], also went in, and **he saw and believed** (John 20:8).

What did he perceive that Peter seemed to have missed?

First of all, the presence of the grave cloths was a glaring clue something most unusual had happened. It was highly improbable someone would have taken the time to unwrap the corpse. A guard, after all, had been placed outside (Matt 27:62–66, #168). In the unlikely event that someone was able to sneak into the tomb unnoticed, why risk taking valuable time to remove the grave cloths from the lifeless corpse?

It wasn't just the presence of the grave cloths that enlivened the faith of the "other disciple." He also noticed the position of the head scarf that had covered Jesus' head. It was carefully folded up where the head had been.

When Lazarus was raised from the dead, he too had a head scarf on his head, but he came walking out of the tomb with it wrapped around his head (John 11:44, #118). Jesus' head scarf was carefully folded. Seeing it that way compelled John to accept that Jesus was raised from the dead and alive.

Seeing is Believing

He [John] **saw** the linen cloths lying there.

—John 20:5

He [Peter] **saw** the linen cloths lying there.

—John 20:6

Both Peter and John saw the same evidence. But only one of them (John) "saw and believed" (John 20:8).

Post-Resurrection Appearances (#173–183)

Mark 16:9–18
Luke 24:13–49
John 20:11–21:25
Acts 1:3–8
1 Cor 15:5–7

No one had actually seen Jesus alive. The empty tomb and the angelic messengers had testified to his resurrection. But as of yet, Jesus had not revealed himself to anyone. That was about to change. Jesus would make five separate post-resurrection appearances on Sunday, the "third day" since he was crucified (Figure 81). The appearances all took place in or around Jerusalem.

Jesus first appeared to Mary Magdalene (#173) followed shortly by the other women who started the day wanting to bury him properly (#174). Then, he had a private encounter with Peter, his wayward apostle (this occurred between #174–176). Later that day, Jesus appeared to two other disciples along the road from Jerusalem to Emmaus (#176). They ran back to Jerusalem and excitedly told the apostles about their experience. Jesus then made an appearance to the apostles, too (#178).

Jesus' Sunday Post-Resurrection Appearances

Name	Timeframe	Citation	Section
1. Mary Magdalene	Early morning, around 7 A.M.	Mark 16:9; John 20:14	#173
2. The Women	Early morning, soon after	Matt 28:9–10	#174
3. Peter	Unknown	Luke 24:34	between #174–176
4. The Two on the Road to Emmaus	Early evening, before 6 P.M.	Luke 24:13, 29	#176
5. The Ten Apostles	After sundown, around 8 P.M.	Mark 16:14; Luke 24:36; John 19:19	#178

Figure 81.

Mark 16:9–11
John 20:11–18

Appearance to Mary Magdalene (#173)

After Peter and John left the tomb, Mary Magdalene remained, standing outside. Crying, confused, and no doubt very frightened, she stooped to look into the tomb. Inside were the two angels she and the other women had talked with earlier (#171).

> And she saw two angels in white, sitting where the body of Jesus had lain, one at the head and one at the feet (John 20:12).

"There I will meet with you…from above the mercy seat, from between the two cherubim [angels] that are on the ark of the testimony."

—Ex 25:22

John's account tells us the angels are on either side of where Jesus' body had lain. The position of the angels in the tomb was reminiscent of the position of the angels on the Ark of the Covenant (cf. Ex 25:22). This detail of the angels' position in the tomb was a subtle, but powerful, testimony to the deity of Jesus. Even as God would appear between the two angels on the Ark of the Covenant, so Jesus too had been between where the two angels now sat.

Peter and John hadn't seen the angels, but they reappeared for Mary Magdalene.

> They [the angels] said to her, "Woman, why are you weeping?" She said to them, "They have taken away my Lord, and I do not know where they have laid him" (John 20:13).

Mary heard the angels tell her Jesus' body was no longer here and that he was alive. In fact, it was not long ago that she and several other women had been told this news by the angels (#171). But her grief would not permit her to accept their assurances.

After saying, "I do not know where they have laid him," Mary suddenly turned around. What caused her to do this?

- Perhaps the angels shifted their eyes from her to the person behind her. They might have even pointed toward him.
- Mary might have heard someone walk up behind her.

Curiously, the text does not say. Regardless, she turned around and saw Jesus—but did not recognize him.

He asked her the same question the angels had asked, "Woman, why are you weeping?" (John 20:13, 15). He added, "Who are you seeking?" But Jesus knew exactly for whom she was looking: She was trying to find *him*.

> Jesus said to her, "Woman, why are you weeping? Whom are you seeking?" Supposing him to be the gardener, she said to him, "Sir, if you have carried him away, tell me where you have laid him, and I will take him away" (John 20:15).

Mary didn't recognize Jesus and assumed he must be the gardener. Joseph of Arimathea's private cemetery would have had a caretaker. Who else would be there so early in the morning? Still believing Jesus was dead, she pleaded with him to tell her where Jesus' body was. "Sir, I will take him away," she said.

She desperately wanted to find Jesus.

And then, the "gardener" called Mary by her name. He said it in such a way that made her suddenly realize this was Jesus (cf. John 10:3, #101a).

> Jesus said to her, "Mary." She turned and said to him in Aramaic, "Rabboni!" (John 20:16). Jesus said to her, "Do not cling to me,

"Rabboni"

Today, the word "Rabbi" denotes a Jewish leader. In Jesus' day, it was a respectful term that meant "Teacher."

Rabboni (pronounced rab-BOW-nigh) was another form of this word.

> for I have not yet ascended to the Father; but go to my brothers and say to them, 'I am ascending to my Father and your Father, to my God and your God' " (John 20:17).

He called them his "brothers" (cf. Matt 28:10, #174). Previously, he had called the disciples his "friends" (John 15:14, #150a). After the resurrection, everything changed. Although Jesus was the Son of God, his disciples were now his brothers and sisters.

We are the adopted children of God (cf. Gal 4:4–6). As his sons and daughters, we are the recipients of all God's spiritual blessings in Christ (Eph 1:5).

Jesus maintains a unique relationship with the Father that we do not. He said, "*My* father and *your* Father" and "*my* God and *your* God" (John 20:17). Later, Thomas would confess Jesus as "*my* Lord and *my* God" (John 20:28, #179). We today confess our faith in Jesus to be the Son of God, too (cf. Rom 10:9).

Mary Magdalene had been present at Jesus' death (Mark 15:40), his burial (Mark 15:47) and then his resurrection. In fact, she had the privilege of being the first person to see the resurrected Lord. Her example of faithfulness and love serves as a wonderful testimony to us today.

Matt 28:9–10

Appearance to the Other Women (#174)

It seems Mary had stayed behind while the other women ran straight to the apostles, informing them about the empty tomb (#172). Some time later that morning, however, Jesus also appeared to the other women. He walked right up to them and said, "Greetings!" This common expression was one of his first spoken words after his resurrection (see Figure 82).

The disciples immediately recognized Jesus. In their excitement, they "took hold of his feet and worshiped him" (Matt 28:9). This act of homage showed their respect and adoration reserved only for God. He comforted them with the same words that the angels had told them earlier: "Do not be afraid (see Matt 28:5).* Fear has been replaced with joy.

---

* Every post-resurrection appearance of Jesus is recorded in #173–184 (#175 is not a post-resurrection appearance, however). Here at the end of

Jesus' Last Words Before His Death on the Cross and His First Words After His Resurrection

Last Words on the Cross		First Words After His Resurrection	
"My God, my God, why have you forsaken me?"	Matt 27:46	"Greetings!"	Matt 28:9
"My God, my God, why have you forsaken me?"	Mark 15:34	"Go into all the world and proclaim the gospel…"	Mark 16:15
"Father, into your hands I commit my spirit!"	Luke 23:46	"What is this conversation that you are holding…?"	Luke 24:17
"It is finished!"	John 19:30	"Why are you weeping? Whom are you seeking?"	John 20:15

Figure 82.

Appearance to Peter Alone (between #174–176)

In piecing together the vivid post-resurrection accounts across all four Gospels, it was apparent that, at some point during Resurrection Sunday, Jesus met privately with Peter. We know this because, later in the day when two disciples told the apostles about their experience with Jesus, they mentioned that "the Lord…has appeared to Simon [i.e., Peter]" (Luke 24:34; see #176 below).

The angels had singled out Peter when they told the women about Jesus' resurrection. They had said, "Go, tell his disciples *and Peter…*" (Mark 16:7). The reconciliation between Jesus and Peter would not be completed until much later (John 21:15–19, #180), but it was touching that, before appearing to all the other disciples, Jesus took the time to seek out Peter, his friend, who had failed him (#156).

---

his Gospel account, Matthew has only recorded Jesus' appearance to the other women (#174) and the meeting in Galilee (#181), omitting all the others (#173, 176–180, 182–184).

According to Matt 28:10, Jesus told the women he wanted his disciples (he calls them his "brothers") to meet him in *Galilee*. Then, after (Matt 28:11–15, #175), we are told "the eleven disciples went to *Galilee*, to the mountain which Jesus had directed them" (Matt 28:16, #181). This meeting, however, would not actually occur for several more weeks (cf. Acts 1:3, #183).

Matt 28:11–15

The Soldiers Report to the Religious Leaders (#175)

The religious leaders had sealed the tomb and posted a guard because they wanted to prevent Jesus' body from being stolen (Matt 27:62–66, #168). They must have been distraught when the soldiers came to them and told them about the earthquake and the missing body of Jesus.

The priests immediately went into damage control mode. They bribed the guards with both money and assurances that efforts would be made to protect them from Pilate, if the governor ever found out about the breach.

But the religious leaders needed them to do something in return. Because the body of Jesus was clearly missing, some sort of plausible explanation had to be provided, otherwise people would start to believe Jesus had indeed been resurrected from the dead. The priests commissioned the guards to spread the rumor that the disciples of Jesus had stolen the body at night while the soldiers were asleep.

The evidence of Jesus' resurrection speaks against this rumor. The large stone at the mouth of the tomb was sealed. Opening it would have made enough noise to awaken any sleeping guards. Also, it is unlikely that untrained Galileans would be capable of outmaneuvering a group of well-trained soldiers.

To complicate matters, it is illogical to think that these men who sacrificed everything, including their own lives, would steal Jesus' body and then lie about it, telling everyone Jesus was raised from the dead. Rather, these men, who were eyewitnesses of these events, were fully convinced of the resurrection.

The eyewitness testimony across the four Gospels shows signs of authenticity. Piecing together the numerous post-resurrection appearances shows that these inspired authors did not collude together before penning these vivid and detailed accounts. Instead, they are telling us what really happened that amazing Sunday. Jesus rose from the dead, and many different people saw him.

Appearance to the Two Disciples on the Road from Jerusalem to Emmaus (#176)

Mark 16:12–13
Luke 24:13–32

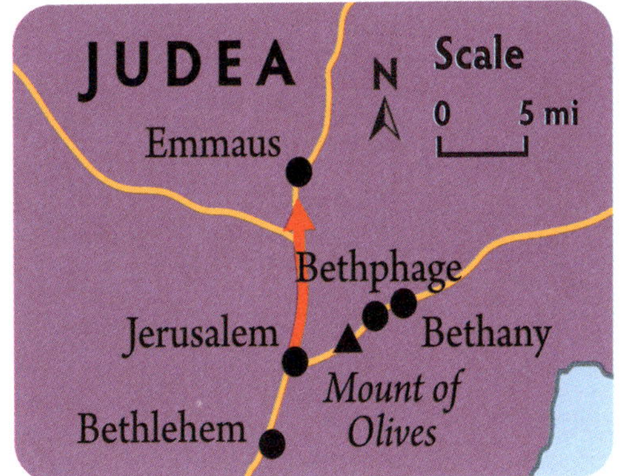

In the late afternoon, two of the disciples, Cleopas and his friend (the other one is not named), left the secret location in Jerusalem and started heading back home to Emmaus, a small village about seven miles to the northwest. Dejected and sad, they were talking with each other along the road when a stranger joined them. They had no idea it was Jesus (Luke 24:16; see Figure 83), who engaged with them about the recent events.

> And [Jesus] said to them, "What is this conversation that you are holding with each other as you walk?" And they stood still, looking sad. Then one of them, named Cleopas, answered him, "Are you the only visitor to Jerusalem who does not know the things that have happened there in these days?" And he said to them, "What things?" (Luke 24:17–19a).

Three Times When the Resurrected Jesus Was Not Recognized

Name	Citation	Citation
Mary Magdalene	She did not know that it was Jesus.	John 20:14
The two on the road to Emmaus	Their eyes were kept from recognizing him.	Luke 24:16; cf. Mark 16:12
The seven disciples fishing	The disciples did not know that it was Jesus.	John 21:4

Figure 83.

Jesus wanted to hear their unvarnished perspective. They briefly recounted the trial and crucifixion of Jesus, placing the blame squarely on the shoulders of the religious leaders. They further revealed their hopes in Jesus to "redeem Israel" were dashed by his death (Luke 24:20). "It is now the third day since these things happened" (Luke 24:21), they added. To make matters worse, the recent report of the empty tomb and the presence of angels had left them confused and startled.*

* These two disciples apparently missed the additional report by the women that they later actually saw the resurrected Jesus.

> "Some of those who were with us went to the tomb and found it just as the women had said, but him they did not see" (Luke 24:24).

"Him they did not see." What these two disciples did not see just yet was how they were now witnesses of his resurrection, too. They also failed to realize Jesus has indeed redeemed Israel—and all the world—by dying on the cross (cf. Matt 20:28; 1 Tim 2:6).

When Jesus took his turn in the conversation, he rebuked them.

> And he said to them, "O foolish ones, and slow of heart to believe all that the prophets have spoken! Was it not necessary that the Christ should suffer these things and enter into his glory?" And beginning with Moses and all the Prophets, he interpreted to them in all the Scriptures the things concerning himself (Luke 24:25–27).

He talked with them until they finally arrived at Emmaus. With the sun setting, they urged this "stranger" to stay with them. When they sat down to eat their evening meal, Jesus took the bread and blessed it. He then broke it and started handing the broken pieces to them. And then, suddenly, they realized it was Jesus.

> And their eyes were opened, and they recognized him. And he vanished from their sight (Luke 24:31).

After recognizing Jesus and then witnessing his miraculous departure, these two disciples could hardly contain their excitement.

> They said to each other, "Did not our hearts burn within us while he talked to us on the road, while he opened to us the Scriptures?" (Luke 24:32).

They immediately made the seven-mile trip back to Jerusalem as quickly as they could. They had to tell the apostles about their amazing experience.

Luke 24:33–35
1 Cor 15:5a

Report of the Two Disciples to the Rest (#177)

The two disciples made their way from Emmaus back to the secret gathering place of the disciples. This was the second time for them to be there that day, the Resurrection Sunday. But now, they had their own amazing report to relay. Jesus is alive!

Their credibility was bolstered by Peter's testimony, too (Luke 24:34). He also had seen the resurrected Jesus.

And then, they all did.

Appearance to the Ten Apostles (#178)

Mark 16:14
Luke 24:36–43
John 20:19–25

While discussing this newest sighting of Jesus, the disciples were greeted by him as he suddenly stood among them. What made this more startling was the room they were in was locked. Miraculously, Jesus had made his way inside (John 20:19).

At first, they thought he was some sort of apparition. Because their hearts were still filled with doubt, they struggled to believe their eyes. Jesus rebuked them for their lack of faith.

> "Why are you troubled, and why do doubts arise in your hearts? See my hands and my feet, that it is I myself. Touch me, and see. For a spirit does not have flesh and bones as you see that I have" (John 20:38–39).

He showed them his resurrected body, which bore the marks of his crucifixion, the imprints of the nails in his hands and his feet. And yet, Jesus was strong and whole. "A spirit does not have flesh and bones as you see I have," he told them (Luke 24:39). To remove any further doubt, he ate a piece of broiled fish in front of them (Luke 24:42–43). Only a real person could do that. With their hearts filled with a mixture of fear and excitement, the disciples rejoiced. The reports were true. Jesus was alive! And at the close of this Resurrection Sunday, they had finally seen him.

All but one of them, that is. For some reason, Thomas was not with the disciples that evening and refused to take his fellow 10 apostles at their word.

> "Unless I see in his hands the mark of the nails... and place my hand into his side, I will never believe" (John 20:25).

He would have to wait an entire week before seeing Jesus for himself (#179, John 20:26). Apparently, Jesus made no post-resurrection appearances until the following Sunday.

The Eleven

When Judas committed suicide, the **twelve** apostles were called briefly the **eleven** (Mark 16:14; Luke 24:9, 33; cf. Acts 2:14).

In Luke 24:9, 33, it is actually the "Ten," since Thomas was not with them (see #178, John 20:24–25). But since Thomas' absence was never mentioned in Luke's account, the "Ten" are called the "Eleven."

Thomas missed more that evening than just the opportunity to see the resurrected Jesus. He failed to be part of a special moment when Jesus commissioned his apostles for the first time after his resurrection (John 20:22–23). Additionally, he missed out on the fulfillment of two promises Jesus made to the apostles in his Farewell Discourse (John 14–16). On the previous Thursday, he told them, "I will come to you" (John 14:18, #149) and "you will see me" (John 16:16, #150d). When it happened, though, Thomas wasn't there. But he would have a second chance (Figure 84).

Fulfilled Promises Jesus Made to the Apostles

Promise	Promise Citation	Fulfillment without Thomas	Fulfillment with Thomas
"I will not leave you as orphans; I will come to you."	John 14:18	John 20:19	John 20:26
"A little while, and you will see me."	John 16:16b	John 20:20	John 20:27
"But the Helper, the Holy Spirit…the Father will send in my name…"	John 14:26	John 20:22	Acts 2:1–4

Figure 84.

John 20:26–31
1 Cor 15:5b

Appearance to the Eleven Apostles (#179)

On the following Sunday ("eight days later"), the apostles—this time including Thomas—were huddled together in their secret location in Jerusalem. Suddenly, Jesus appeared among them, despite the locked doors. After greeting them, Jesus turned his focus to Thomas, challenging his doubting disciple to place his hands on Jesus' scars. "Do not disbelieve, but believe" (John 20:27).

"Eight Days Later"

According to John 20:26, Thomas saw Jesus "eight days later."

This would have included the Resurrection Sunday and the following week (from Sunday to Sunday).

Because of his initial skepticism, Thomas has become known as "doubting Thomas." In his defense, he demanded to see only the same evidence the other apostles did, too (Luke 24:38–40, #178). Upon seeing Jesus, he exclaimed, "My Lord and my God!" No Jew would say these words to a mere mortal. Having seen his resurrected Lord, Thomas was convinced that Jesus was truly God.

It was only *after* Thomas saw the resurrected Lord he made this magnificent confession. On the previous Sunday, John ("the other disciple") came away from the empty tomb believing in Jesus *before* he saw the resurrected Jesus (John 20:8, #172). Jesus responded to Thomas' confession by praising those who, in the future, would believe in his resurrection without having seen him.

> Jesus said to him, "Have you believed because you have seen me? Blessed are those who have not seen and yet have believed" (John 20:28–29; see also 1 Pet 1:8).

Jesus was talking about us today who have not seen him physically, but still believe in the overwhelming evidence of his resurrection, including the eyewitness testimony of his disciples (Luke 1:2, #1). The purpose of the four Gospels is to provide this evidence, so we will believe it and have eternal life (John 20:30–31).

Appearances to Seven Disciples While Fishing (#180)

John 21:1–25

In keeping with Jesus' instructions, the disciples made their way back to Galilee (cf. Matt 28:9, #174). While waiting for Jesus to appear again, Peter grew restless. "I am going fishing," he told the others. As a professional fisherman, he worked the shores of the Sea of Galilee (called "the Sea of Tiberias in v. 1) countless times. Peter was joined by six others, including James and John ("the sons of Zebedee"), Thomas and Nathanael.*

They fished all night and caught absolutely nothing. In the morning, they were approached by a potential customer who asked them, "Children, do you have any fish?" In their frustration, they gave him a one-word answer: "No."

> He said to them, "Cast the net on the right side of the boat, and you will find some." So they cast it, and now they were not able to haul it in, because of the quantity of fish (John 21:6).

All of a sudden, their nets were full of 153 squirming large fish. Even more remarkably, their nets did not break, despite the great quantity of fish they took in.

MIRACLE 38 (see Sec. 41)
The Second Catch of Fish

---

* The two additional disciples are speculated to be Andrew and Philip. This is because the Gospel of John began with Andrew and Philip introducing Peter (then Simon) and Nathanael to Jesus (John 1:40, 43, #28).

John experienced a moment of *déjà vu*. He remembered he and Peter, along with Andrew and James, had spent all night fishing in these very waters three years prior (Luke 5:3–11, #41). After a disappointing night, *when they had caught nothing,* it was Jesus who came along and told them where to cast their nets. And when they did, those nets were suddenly and miraculously full of fish.

> **"A Charcoal Fire"**
>
> Now the servants and officers had made a charcoal fire.... Peter also was with them, standing and warming himself.
>
> —John 18:18
>
> When they got out on land, they saw a charcoal fire in place, with fish laid out on it, and bread.
>
> —John 20:6

When Peter denied Jesus, he was next to a charcoal fire. It is present again as he takes back those denials.

John turned to Peter and said, "It is the Lord!" As at other times during Jesus' post-resurrection appearances, they had been prevented from recognizing him (v. 14; see John 20:14, #173; Luke 24:16, #176). But they just knew it was Jesus. They had no doubts about it.

Peter put on his outer garment, dove into the water, and started swimming. Unwilling to wait, he swam the hundred yards to shore. That's how excited he was to see his friend, Jesus, again.

Jesus already had a charcoal fire burning (cf. John 18:18, #156) with cooked fish and bread laid out. He asked them to bring some of their fish, too, and eat breakfast with him.

Jesus was nearing the time when he would ascend back to the Father. But, he and Peter had some unfinished business they needed to address. Peter had denied three times he even knew Jesus (#156). Jesus, in front of the others, asked Peter a question (Figure 85). He didn't address him as Peter, but instead addressed him as Simon, as if they're going back to the beginning of their relationship and starting over afresh.

Peter Takes Back His Three Denials (John 21:15–17)

Jesus' Question	Peter's Answer	Jesus' Response	Citation
1. "Simon, son of John, do you love me more than these?"	"Yes, Lord; you know that I love you."	"Feed my lambs."	v. 15
2. "Simon, son of John, do you love me?"	"Yes, Lord; you know that I love you."	"Tend my sheep."	v. 16
3. "Simon, son of John, do you love me?"	Grieved, Peter answered: "Lord, you know everything; you know that I love you."	"Feed my sheep."	v. 17

Figure 85.

"Simon, son of John, do you love me more than these?" he asked him. *Does Peter love Jesus?* Of course, he did. And Peter answered Jesus without hesitation.

> [Peter] said to him, "Yes, Lord; you know that I love you." He said to him, "Feed my lambs" (v. 15).

But Jesus wasn't finished yet. He asked Peter the question again, but the phrase "more than these" was left off. Peter answered Jesus with the exact same words.*

> He said to him, "Yes, Lord; you know that I love you." He said to him, "Tend my sheep" (v. 16).

Then, Jesus asked him a third time. Doing so distressed Peter terribly because he knew exactly what Jesus was doing. He was giving him the opportunity to take back each of his three denials. Peter was forced to relive that moment in Caiaphas' courtyard when he had failed his friend.

Jesus let Peter take back his third and final denial from that fateful night. Jesus proceeded to tell his newly restored apostle that one day, he would die a martyr's death. In the garden of Gethsemane, Peter had said, "Even if I must die with you, I will not deny you!" (Matt 26:35, #147). The next time he was surrounded by enemies, Peter would be ready (cf. 1 Pet 3:15; 2 Pet 1:14).

Jesus always had known Peter was going to return to him (Luke 22:32, #147). In fact, Jesus knew that, though all of his disciples fled in fear that night in the garden, they would all return to him, except Judas (John 17:12, #151). And Jesus forgave them freely.

Throughout this closing account in John's Gospel, it was not Peter's failure but Jesus' forgiveness that was being emphasized. Having died for the sins of humanity, Jesus will forgive us, too.

---

* It is often pointed out that there are two different Greek verbs translated "love" in John 21:15–17. John's Gospel uses different words with similar meanings interchangeably and these distinctions are not always visible in English translations. Likely, the different verbs are for stylistic purposes, and there is not a hidden meaning in Jesus' words to Peter.

Matt 28:16–20
Mark 16:15–18
1 Cor 15:6

Appearance to the Eleven In Galilee (#181)

Over a period of 40 days, Jesus appeared to his apostles in both Galilee and Jerusalem. He spent a great deal of time instructing them about their future work of preaching the gospel. They were to take the message to the entire world.

The instructions Jesus gave them are commonly referred to as the Great Commission (Figure 86). The Limited Commission (#70) focused on evangelizing among the Jewish people only, but after the resurrection, the apostles were instructed to "make disciples of all nations" (Matt 28:19).

The Great Commission

Jesus' Commission	Citation
"Go therefore and make disciples of all nations, baptizing them in the name of the Father and of the Son and of the Holy Spirit."	Matt 28:18–20 (#181)
"Go into all the world and proclaim the gospel to the whole creation."	Mark 16:15–16 (#181)
"Repentance for the forgiveness of sins should be proclaimed in his name to all nations, beginning from Jerusalem. You are witnesses of these things."	Luke 24:44–48 (#183)
"Peace be with you. As the Father has sent me, even so I am sending you."	John 20:21–23 (#179)

Figure 86.

The Great Commission was the result of everything Jesus had-been working toward. After he left and returned to the Father, the Holy Spirit would be sent to guide the apostles on this Great Commission (John 16:13, #150c). The exponential growth of the church of Jesus Christ unfolded in the Book of Acts.

As he began the Great Commission, Jesus declared he held "all authority in heaven and on earth" (Matt 28:18). The kingdom of God had at last been established throughout the world, just as it was in heaven (cf. Matt 6:10, #54f). God is honored as King when his royal subjects receive salvation and live their lives dependent upon his love and providence (cf. 2 Cor 5:7).

Jesus promised to be with his followers forever when he said, "I am with you always" (Matt 28:20). He is Immanuel, which means "God is with us" (Matt 1:23, #9).

Jesus is still with us today and always will be.

Appearance to James, Jesus' Brother (#182)

1 Cor 15:7

During Jesus' ministry, members of his own family did not believe in him (cf. Mark 3:21, #61; John 7:5, #94). Yet, something happened to change their minds. James, the half-brother of Jesus, became a great leader in the New Testament church (Acts 12:17; 15:13; 21:18; Gal 2:9). With the simple statement, "he appeared to James," Paul let us know Jesus made a post-resurrection appearance to his brother, and that changed everything.

James was likely the author of the letter that bears his name, even though he identified himself only as "a slave of God and of the Lord Jesus Christ" (James 1:1). Many scholars believe James's letter was written in the early A.D. 40s, which would make it the first New Testament document ever written.

According to the Jewish historian, Josephus, "James, the brother of Jesus, who was called the Messiah," was executed by the Sadducean high priest Annus II in A.D. 62 (*Ant.*, 20.200). James, the brother of Jesus, died a martyr's death because of his faith in Jesus to be the Christ, the Son of God.

Appearance to the Disciples In Jerusalem (#183)

Luke 24:44–49
Acts 1:3–8

The Book of Acts continued the story of the Gospels. Luke wrote both the Gospel of Luke and the Book of Acts, which began where the Gospel of Luke left off. Under the guidance of the Holy Spirit, the church and its message spread throughout the world.

Jesus continued to meet with his apostles and teach them until the moment of his ascension (#184). In his teaching, he reminded them how his suffering on the cross and his triumphant resurrection from the dead had been necessary (Luke 24:46–47). The message of salvation would be proclaimed to the entire world.

Mark 16:19–20
Luke 24:50–53
Acts 1:9–12

The Ascension (#184)

From atop the Mount of Olives, Jesus told his apostles they would be his "witnesses" in the world (Acts 1:8). With his work on earth completed, Jesus was ready to ascend back to heaven. A cloud enveloped Jesus as he was lifted up and disappeared from view. In this bittersweet moment, Jesus, their friend, was gone.

The disciples were so intently looking up that they didn't notice the sudden appearance of two men dressed in white robes standing alongside them. They were angels sent by God to affirm Jesus' promise to return.

> "Men of Galilee, why do you stand looking into heaven? This Jesus, who was taken up from you into heaven, will come in the same way as you saw him go into heaven" (Acts 1:11).

Conclusion

Paul the apostle gave his life to spreading the gospel all over the known world. A prolific writer, Paul penned numerous letters in the New Testament. In one of his last letters, he wrote a poem about Jesus' ministry and the growth of the church.

> Great indeed, we confess, is the mystery of godliness:
>
> He was manifested in the flesh,
> vindicated by the Spirit,
> seen by angels,
> proclaimed among the nations,
> believed on in the world,
> taken up in glory (1 Tim 3:16).

The Gospels beautifully tell us about what Jesus started. But this is not the end of the story: It is only the beginning. The remainder of the New Testament (Acts–Revelation) reveals the unfolding of God's masterful plan to deliver and nurture the kingdom of God in the hearts of all humanity. This is made perfectly clear in the opening verses of the Book of Acts (Acts 1:1–2). Luke explains that the work of spreading the gospel to all the world was only now getting started.

> In the first book, O Theophilus, I have dealt with all that Jesus began to do and teach, until the day when he was taken up, after

he had given commands through the Holy Spirit to the apostles whom he had chosen (Acts 1:1–2).

"All that Jesus began *to do and teach."* In other words, the Gospels are only the beginning of Jesus' work. While in the Upper Room, Jesus told the apostles he planned to send them "another comforter" who would guide them into all truth (John 14:26–27). Even as Jesus was sent by God, so also was the Holy Spirit.

The ministry of the Holy Spirit recorded in the book of Acts is the continuation of Jesus' ministry recorded in the Gospels. Throughout the book of Acts, the Holy Spirit directly intervened in the events of the early church (Figure 87).

Examples of the Holy Spirit's Intervention in Acts

Acts of the Holy Spirit	Citation
Empowered the apostles and gave them the ability to speak in foreign languages	Acts 2:4; cf. 1:8
Enabled the disciples to preach with boldness	Acts 4:31
Instructed Philip the evangelist to approach the Ethiopian eunuch's chariot	Acts 4:29
Called Barnabas and Saul to preach the gospel in Galatia	Acts 13:2
Directed Paul and Silas away from Asia toward Europe	Acts 16:6

Figure 87.

Luke and Acts are closely linked together. They show us how the disciples imitated Jesus and walked in his footsteps.

- They would perform many of the same miracles (Luke 5:17–26; Acts 3:1–10).
- Even as Jesus journeyed to Jerusalem, so also did Paul (Luke 9:51; Acts 20:22).
- Like Jesus, Paul was seized by a mob (Luke 22:54; Acts 21:30), slapped in the face (Luke 22:63–64; Acts 23:2) and repeatedly declared innocent (Luke 23:4, 14, 22; Acts 23:9; 25:5; 26:31).

We, like they, are walking in Jesus' footsteps. We are imitating him and striving to be like him in every way (Rom 8:29).

God our Father, Jesus, and the Holy Spirit providentially guide us, and the gospel story continues to unfold in our lives. That's because our relationship with Jesus doesn't start when we get to heaven. It begins right now.

- As our high priest, he serves as our intercessor to God (Rom 8:34; Heb 4:14–16; 7:25).
- As King of kings and Lord of lords (Rev 17:14; 19:16), he rules his spiritual kingdom even now (1 Cor 15:25).
- As our ultimate example, he serves as our greatest encourager (Heb 12:1–2).
- As our Savior, he has proven his love for us. And he has prepared a place for us in the heart of God (John 14:2).

In the meantime, Jesus is *always* with us. "I am with you always . . ." is a promise from Immanuel, "God with us," to you and me. He will never leave us or forsake us (Heb 13:5).

WHAT DID YOU LEARN IN LESSON 15?

Match the key concept in the numbered list below with the letter of the phrase that best describes it. Answers appear upside-down at the bottom of the page.

Key Concepts

1. Emmaus
2. Thomas
3. Acts
4. James
5. Great Commission
6. Ascension
7. Empty tomb
8. Mary Magdalene
9. Three days
10. The Eleven
11. Forty days
12. Sunday

Descriptions

A. The term used in reference to the 12 apostles after Judas committed suicide.

B. The length of time Jesus stayed on the earth after his resurrection.

C. The book of the Bible that continues to ministry of Jesus after his ascension.

D. The day of the week when Jesus was resurrected.

E. The first person to see the resurrected Jesus.

F. An event that took Jesus away physically from his disciples. It occurred on top of the Mount of Olives.

G. A town Jesus walked along with two disciples after his resurrection.

H. Jesus' instructions to the apostles just before he physically left them. He told them to preach the gospel to the world.

I. The half-brother of Jesus who became a believer after Jesus' resurrection from the dead.

J. The apostle who doubted Jesus had been raised from the dead.

K. The number of days Jesus said he would be in the tomb.

L. What the disciples saw when they came to visit Jesus' dead body on the day after the Sabbath.

Answers

1G, 2J, 3C, 4I, 5H, 6F, 7L, 8E, 9K, 10A, 11B, 12D

WHAT DID YOU LEARN IN LESSON 15?

Do your best to answer the following questions. Some answers can be found in the text of Lesson 15, but not all of them. For others, you will be asked to look up passages in your Bible to find them.

Fill in the Blanks.

1. After Jesus' resurrection, an angel told the women, "He has __________; he is not here. See where they __________ him" (Mark 15:6).

2. Jesus told Mary Magdalene to report to his disciples, "I am ascending to __________ Father and __________ Father, to __________ God and __________ God" (John 20:13).

3. Thomas said, "Unless I see in his __________ the mark of the __________, and place my __________ into the mark of the __________, and place my hand into his __________, I will never __________" (John 20:25).

4. Three times, Peter said to Jesus, "Yes, Lord, you __________ that I __________ you" (John 21:15–17).

5. When Jesus told his disciples to "make disciples of all nations," he was giving them the __________ Commission (Matt 28:18–20, #181).

6. Jesus guided the apostles during his earthly ministry. Who guided them as they continued Jesus' ministry in the book of Acts? ____________________

7. When Jesus appeared to the 10 apostles, which two were missing? __________ and __________.

Multiple Choice. Circle the correct answer.

1. Why did the women wait until Sunday morning to anoint Jesus' body?
   - A. They couldn't go because of the Sabbath.
   - B. They weren't sure where the tomb was located.
   - C. They didn't have the right kind of spices.
   - D. They were scared to go to the tomb.
2. Who was the first person to see Jesus after he was raised from the dead (not the empty tomb, but Jesus himself)?
   - A. Joseph of Arimathea.
   - B. Peter and John.
   - C. The apostles without Judas or Thomas.
   - D. Mary Magdalene.
3. What was Peter doing the last time he saw Jesus before his crucifixion?
   - A. Praying.
   - B. Preaching.
   - C. Singing hymns.
   - D. Denying Jesus three times.
4. Paul says in 1 Cor 15:7 that Jesus appeared to James. This is a reference to which James in the New Testament?
   - A. The apostle James, the brother of John.
   - B. James the son of Alphaeus.
   - C. James, the father of Judas Iscariot.
   - D. James, the brother of Jesus.
5. When Jesus appeared to Cleopas and his companion on the road to Emmaus, where had they just come from?
   - A. Bethany.
   - B. Bethlehem.
   - C. Jerusalem.
   - D. The high priest's palace.

APPLICATION OF LESSON 15.

For Discussion.

1. What passages from the Old Testament do you think Jesus might have shared with the disciples on the road to Emmaus?

2. Explain the significance of Jesus' last promise to his apostles before his ascension: "I am with you always" (Matt 28:20) and in what way you think this promise is meant for us today.

3. Jesus is our prophet, high priest and king. Explain the significance of each of these roles.

GLOSSARY

A

Acts. The companion volume to the Gospel of Luke.

Akeldama. "Field of Blood." A field outside Jerusalem purchased with the 30 pieces of silver Judas returned to the chief priests (Matt 27:3–10; Acts 1:18–19, #158). Instead of being returned to the temple treasury, the money was used to purchase this field to bury strangers.

Annas. Ruled as high priest from A.D. 6–15, but still clung to power through his son-in-law, Caiaphas, who served during Jesus' ministry.

Apostle. One of Jesus' disciples who was part of his inner circle. The word "apostle" denotes one who is sent. These twelve men were trained by Jesus to go into all the world and carry the gospel message after his ascension.

Arimathea. See **Joseph of Arimathea**.

B

Barabbas. An insurrectionist against Roman rule and a murderer (Matt 27:16; Mark 15:7; Luke 23:19, 25; John 18:40, #161). When Pilate, the prefect of Judea, offered either Jesus or Barabbas be released as a tradition during the Passover, he was surprised the crowd demanded Barabbas be freed instead of the innocent Jesus.

Bethany. A village located two miles east of Jerusalem near the road to Jericho (Mark 11:1). Lazarus and his sisters, Mary and Martha, lived here (John 11).

Bethany beyond the Jordan. A village near the Jordan River where John the Baptist was baptizing (John 1:28, #26). There are two disputed locations (see Map 1 on page 25); the southern location is also referred to as Bethabara.

C

Caiaphas, Joseph. The high priest who presided over Jesus' trial. He was instrumental in having Jesus brought before the Romans.

Calvary. The name of the hill just outside the city of Jerusalem where Jesus was crucified. The term "Calvary" is from the Latin word *calvaria*, "the skull." Sometimes it is called Mount Calvary, but not in the New Testament. The term "Golgotha" (Aramaic for "the skull") refers to the same hill.

Centurion. A commander of 100 Roman soldiers. Two centurions are mentioned in the Gospels: A centurion in Capernaum demonstrated strong faith in Jesus by asking him to heal his servant from a distance (Matt 8:5–13; Luke 7:2–10, #55). Another centurion proclaimed Jesus to be the Son of God after he died (Mark 15:39; Luke 23:47, #166).

Chief Priests. Members of the high priestly family of Annas and Caiaphas, his son-in-law. "Chief priests" and "high priest(s)" are translated from the same Greek word; English translations render it differently depending on the context. See **High Priest**.

Cleopas. One of two disciples the resurrected Jesus appeared to while on the road to Emmaus (Luke 24:18, #176). His companion is never named.

Crown of thorns. Roman soldiers weaved a thorny plant into a circular shape and placed it on Jesus' head during his flogging (Matt 27:29; Mark 15:17; John 19:2, #161). It was intended to mock Jesus' claim to be a king.

Crucifixion. A cruel means of torture inflicted frequently throughout the Roman Empire. The Gospels detail the events leading up to Jesus' crucifixion, but say very little about the crucifixion itself (Matt 27:35; Mark 15:24; Luke; John 19:18, #164).

D

Day of Preparation of the Passover. "The day of preparation" was used as a technical term for the Friday before the Sabbath (Matt 27:62, #168; Mark 15:42, #167a; Luke 23:54, #167b). John's Gospel, however, specifies the day of Jesus' death as the "the day of Preparation of the Passover" (John 19:14, #161). This detail pinpoints Jesus' crucifixion as taking place on a Friday.

Denouement. A literary term that refers to how a story's loose ends are resolved at the end.

Diatessaron. An early attempt to harmonize the records of Jesus' life contained in Matthew, Mark, Luke and John. It literally means "through the four."

The Disciple Whom Jesus Loved. The apostle John's way of referring to himself in his Gospel (John 19:26; 20:2; 21:7, 20; see also John 21:24). He also referred to himself as the "other disciple" (John 18:15–16; 20:2–4, 8) or "that disciple" (John 18:15).

E

Emmaus. A village about seven miles to the northwest of Jerusalem. (The exact location of Emmaus is debated and cannot be definitively pinpointed.) The resurrected Jesus appeared to two disciples as they traveled from Jerusalaem to Emmaus. See **Cleopas**.

Eschatalogical Discourse. See **Olivet Discourse**.

Eusebian Canons. A way derived by ancient Christians to reference similar passages found about Jesus' life. They were first developed by Eusebius (A.D. 263–339).

F

Farewell Discourse. See **Upper Room Discourse**.

Feast of Unleavened Bread. An annual week-long feast that celebrated the day after the Passover in the month of Nisan (which corresponds with our month of April). See **Passover**. See **Nisan**.

Flogging. A severe public whipping of a criminal which is less severe than a scourging. Pilate first flogged Jesus, hoping it would satisfy the religious leaders (John 19:1, #161). After Jesus was condemned to die by crucifixion, he was brutally scourged (Matt 27:26; Mark 15:15, #161). See **Scourging**.

G

Gethsemane. See **Garden of Gethsemane**.

Gentiles. Non-Jews. It literally means "nations" or "people" and refers to anyone who is not an ethnic Jew (a descendant of Abraham through Isaac and Jacob).

Gethsemane. A garden at the base of the Mount of Olives filled with olive trees where Jesus often went with his apostles (cf. John 18:2, #153). Jesus was arrested in this garden (#153). Shortly before his arrest, Jesus prayed three agonizing prayers here (#152).

Golgotha. See **Calvary**.

Gospel. A term that literally means "good news" and is also used to refer to the first four books of the New Testament (Matthew, Mark, Luke and John).

Gospel Harmony. A work that combines the first four books of the New Testament into one seamless story.

Gospel Survey. A book that presents a general view of Jesus' ministry.

Greeks. Non-Jewish believers in Jesus who wanted to see him in Jerusalem (John 12:20–21, #130a).

H

Halekdama. See **Akeldama**.

Hasmonean Palace. The home of the high priest, Annas, and his son-in-law, Caiaphas in the heart of the city of Jerusalem. The Hasmoneans were a dynasty of Jewish high priests and kings who won the independence of Judea during the Maccabean revolt. See **Maccabean Revolt**.

Herod Antipas. The son of Herod the Great who ruled as tetrarch of Galilee. He imprisoned and later beheaded John the Baptist (#71). While in Jerusalem for the Passover, Antipas was asked by Pilate to participate in the Roman Trial of Jesus (Luke 23:7–11, #160).

Herod's Palace. The luxurious palace built by Herod the Great in Jerusalem where Jesus likely stood trial before Pilate (John 18:28, #159; Mark 15:16, #162).

High Priest. Under the Law of Moses, the high priest was to be a direct descendant of Aaron, who was God's first high priest (Deut 10:6). This was also supposed to be a position held for life. This practice was abolished by Herod the Great, who appointed several high priests. Both Annas and Caiaphas are referred to as high priest in the Gospels. See **Annas**. See also **Caiaphas**.

J

Joanna. The wife of Chuza, Herod's household manager. She was one of the women who financially supported Jesus' ministry (Luke 8:3, #60). Joanna was likely one of the women who first saw the empty tomb of Jesus (Luke 24:10, #172).

John. See **Disciple Whom Jesus Loved, The.**

Joseph. The husband of Mary, the mother of Jesus (Matt 1:16, #3; Luke 3:23, #24). He was a carpenter and a direct descendant of King David (Matt 1:20, #3). Joseph was the adoptive father of Jesus, but not his birth father.

Joseph of Arimathea. A member of the Sanhedrin who was a secret disciple of Jesus (John 19:38, #167a). He hurriedly buried Jesus in his own tomb shortly after Jesus' death on the cross (#167b).

Judas Iscariot. The apostle who betrayed Jesus for 30 pieces of silver (Matt 26:14–16, #142). He later returned the money to the chief priests and hanged himself out of remorse (Matt 27:3–10, #158).

Judgment Seat. The seat where Pilate presided over the trial of Jesus (Matt 27:19; John 19:13, #161).

K

Kidron Valley. A valley running along the eastern side of Jerusalem, where the pool of Gihon is located.

L

Last Supper. A term not occurring in the Gospels, but used to describe the last Passover meal Jesus ate with his disciples (#143). It was during this final observance of the Passover that Jesus instituted the Lord's Supper.

Legion. The largest single unit in the Roman army. This term was applied as a moniker for a violent man in Gerasa who was possessed with several demons (Mark 5:9, #66).

Lord's Day. A reference to Sunday. This term is closely associated with Jesus, who was raised from the dead on Sunday (cf. Mark 16:2; Luke 24:1, #171). Its only occurrence in the New Testament in Rev 1:10, however.

Lord's Supper. The term used by Paul in 1 Cor 11:20 to describe the commemorative meal Jesus instituted on the night of his betrayal. Jesus commanded this be eaten in remembrance of his death on the cross (Luke 22:19, #148).

M

Maccabean Revolt. The successful rebellion led by Mattathias Maccabee and his sons started in 167 B.C. to overthrow the Seleucid king of Syria, Antiochus Epiphanes IV. See **Hasmonean Palace.**

Malchus. A slave of the high priest Caiaphas who was present during Jesus' arrest in the Garden of Gethsemane. Peter cut off his ear, but Jesus miraculously restored it (Luke 22:51; John 18:10, #153).

Mary (mother of James and Joses/Joseph). One of several women named Mary in the Gospels. She likely was one of the women who financially assisted Jesus during his ministry (Luke 8:2–3, #60). She was at the cross when Jesus died (Matt 27:56; Mark 15:40, #166), witnessed his burial (Mark 15:47, #168) and came to the empty tomb early on the day Jesus was resurrected (Mark 16:1, #169).

Mary (mother of Jesus). The birth mother of Jesus (Matt 1:16, #3; Matt 1:25, #9). Her husband, Joseph, was not the birth father. See **Joseph**.

Mary (sister of Martha and Lazarus).

Mary (wife of Clopas).

Mary Magdalene. Mary was from Magdala, a town along the shore of the Sea of Galilee. Jesus cast seven demons out of her (Luke 8:2, #60). Mary Magdalene was the first person to see the resurrected Jesus (#173).

Mount of Olives. A small ridge of mountains running north to south along the Kidron Kalley, across from the city of Jerusalem. The high point stands 2,600 feet above sea level. At the foot of the Mount of Olives was the Garden of Gethsemane, where Jesus often went to pray (John 18:2, #153). His triumphal entry began at the Mount of Olives (Matt 21:1, #128b).

N

Nicodemus. A Pharisee and member of the Sanhedrin Council who visited Jesus at night early in his ministry (John 3:1, #32b). Nicodemus and Joseph of Arimathea hurriedly buried Jesus shortly after his death on the cross (#167b).

Nisan. The name of the month during which the Passover occurred. It is roughly equivalent to our late March or early April.

O

Olivet Discourse. One of the longest discourses of Jesus recorded in the Gospels (Matt 24–25, #139). In this extended speech, Jesus predicted the destruction of Jerusalem in A.D. 70 and briefly spoke of his second coming, which is sometimes referred to as his "parousia." Matthew uses the Greek word *parousia* four times in Matt 24 (vv. 3, 27, 37, and 39).

P

Parallel passage. A text or group of verses about Jesus' life and ministry that is very similar to another text or group of verses.

Parousia. The Greek noun for "coming." It is used as a technical term for the second coming of Jesus. See **Olivet Discourse**.

Passion. The last week of Jesus' life prior to his crucifixion. It began on Sunday when he made his triumphal entry into the city of Jerusalem (#128b) and ended with his crucifixion on Friday. The term "passion" is from the Latin root *passio* which means "to suffer."

Plot. The main events of a story that are devised and presented in a sequential and interrelated order.

Passover. One of the annual feasts of the Jews. It commemorated the ancient Israelites' deliverance from Egypt under the leadership of Moses (Ex 12). Jesus was crucified during the Passover (cf. Matt 26:2, #140).

Peter. See Simon Peter.

Pilate, Pontius. The prefect of Judea from A.D. 25–37 who presided over Jesus' trial. He gave into the demands of Caiaphas and had Jesus crucified.

Praetorium. The temporary palace for the Roman prefect, Pontius Pilate (John 18:28, 33, #159; Matt 27:27; Mark 15:16, #162).

Prefect. The term for a Roman governor or procurator. See **Pilate, Pontius**.

S

Sabbath. The seventh day of the week and the day of rest for the Jewish people. Jesus was perceived by the religious leaders to violate the Sabbath by healing on this day.

Salome. One of Jesus' female disciples. She was present at the crucifixion (Mark 15:40) and the empty tomb (Mark 16:1).

Sanhedrin. The highest Jewish tribunal. It was made up of 70 members that included both Pharisees and Sadducees and was headed by the high priest (Caiaphas in the gospels). The Sanhedrin Council met on the second floor of Solomon's Colonnade in the Jerusalem temple.

Scourging. A brutal form of torture implemented by Roman soldiers on their crucifixion victims. Jesus was at first flogged by Pilate, who hoped this would satisfy the religious leaders. When Jesus was condemned to be crucified, he was first scourged (Matt 27:26, #161). See **Flogging**.

Simon (of Cyrene). The father of Alexander and Rufus, who was compelled to carry the cross of Jesus (Matt 27:32; Mark 15:21; Luke 23:26, #163).

Simon Peter. The natural leader among the twelve apostles who is always listed first. He denied Jesus but was restored. Peter may have assisted Mark in writing his Gospel.

Son of Man. Jesus' self-designation in all four gospels, based on Dan 7:13–14, which designates him as God's chosen messenger. When he uses this expression, it is always in the third person.

Synoptic Gospels. A term that refers to Matthew, Mark and Luke apart from the Gospel of John. It literally means "same view."

Synoptic Problem. A term that describes the phenomenon of different words and similar words being used to record the same events in the first four books of the New Testament.

T

Theophilus. The person to whom Luke dedicated his companion volumes, Luke and Acts (Luke 1:1–4, #1; Acts 1:1–2).

Twelve, the. See **Apostle**.

U

Unleavened Bread, Feast of. See **Feast of Unleavened Bread.**

Upper Room. A room built on the roof of a house. Jesus instituted the Lord's Supper in an upper room with his disciples (Luke 22:7–13, #143).

Upper Room Discourse. The last speech Jesus made to his apostles prior to his death on the cross (John 14–16, #149–150).

GENERAL INDEX

G

H

I

J

K

L

R

SCRIPTURE INDEX

Mark

Luke

John

Acts

Romans

1 Corinthians

2 Corinthians

Galatians

Ephesians

Philippians

Colossians

1 Thessalonians

1 Timothy

Titus

Hebrews

James

1 Peter

2 Peter

1 John

Revelation

ANCIENT REFERENCES INDEX

Josephus

Antiquities

Jewish War

13-WEEK GOSPELS READING PLAN

LESSON 3 (#1–19) **33 MINUTES** Two Miraculous Births ca. 6 B.C.–6 A.D.

WEEK 1, DAY 1 **TIME: 9 MINUTES**

#1 . . . . Luke 1:1–4

#2 . . . . John 1:1–18

#3 . . . . Matt 1:1–17; Luke 3:23b–28

WEEK 1, DAY 2 **TIME: 10 MINUTES**

#4–8 . . . . Luke 1:5–80

WEEK 1, DAY 3 **TIME: 14 MINUTES**

#9 . . . . Matt 1:18–25

#10–13 . . . . Luke 2:1–38

#14–19 . . . . Matt 2:1–23; Luke 2:39–52

LESSON 4 (#20–23) **7 MINUTES** John the Baptist's Ministry Spring A.D. 26

WEEK 2, DAY 1 **TIME: 7 MINUTES**

#20–23 . . . . . . Matt 3:1–12; Mark 1:1–8; Luke 3:1–18

LESSON 5: JESUS' MINISTRY BEGINS (#24–30) **13 MINUTES** Jesus' Ministry Begins January–April A.D. 27

WEEK 2, DAY 2 **TIME: 13 MINUTES**

#24–25 . . . . . . Matt 3:13–4:11; Mark 1:9–13; Luke 3:21–23a; 4:1–13

#26–30 . . . . . . John 1:19–2:12

Early Judean Ministry
April A.D. 27

LESSON 6 (#31–36) 16 MINUTES

WEEK 2, DAY 3 TIME: 16 MINUTES

#31–33 . . . . John 2:13–3:36

#34. . . . . John 4:1–4; Luke 3:19–20; Matt 4:12; Mark 1:14a; Luke 4:14a

#35–36. . . . . . . John 4:5–45

Early Galilean Ministry
December A.D. 27–April A.D. 28

LESSON 7 (#37–52) 47 MINUTES

WEEK 3, DAY 1 TIME: 7 MINUTES

#37 . . . . Matt 4:17; Mark 1:14–15; Luke 4:14–15

#38 . . . . John 4:46–54

#39 . . . . Luke 4:16–30

#40 . . . . Matt 4:13–16

WEEK 3, DAY 2 TIME: 14 MINUTES

#41 . . . . Matt 4:18–22; Mark 1:16–20; Luke 5:1–11

#42. . . . . Mark 1:21–28; Luke 4:31–37

#43. . . . . Matt 8:14–17; Mark 1:29–34; Luke 4:38–41

#44 . . . . Matt 4:23–25; Mark 1:35–39; Luke 4:42–44

#45. . . . . Matt 8:2–4; Mark 1:40–45; Luke 5:12–16

WEEK 3, DAY 3 TIME: 11 MINUTES

#46. . . . . Matt 9:1–8; Mark 2:1–12; Luke 5:17–26

#47. . . . . Matt 9:9–13; Mark 2:13–17; Luke 5:27–32

#48. . . . . Matt 9:14–17; Mark 2:18–22; Luke 5:33–39

WEEK 3, DAY 4 TIME: 15 MINUTES

#49..........John 5:1–47

#50..........Matt 12:1–8; Mark 2:23–28; Luke 6:1–5

#51 ....Matt 12:9–14; Mark 3:1–6; Luke 6:6–11

#52..........Matt 12:15–21; Mark 3:7–12

LESSON 8 (#53–71) 1 HOUR, 14 MINUTES

Middle Galilean Ministry
June A.D. 28–February A.D. 29

WEEK 4, DAY 1 TIME: 8 MINUTES

#53..........Mark 3:13–19; Luke 6:12–16

#54..........Luke 6:17–49

WEEK 4, DAY 2 TIME: 17 MINUTES

#54..........Matt 5:1–8:1

WEEK 4, DAY 3 TIME: 16 MINUTES

#55..........Matt 8:5–13; Luke 7:1–10

#56..........Luke 7:11–17

#57..........Matt 11:2–19; Luke 7:18–35

#58..........Matt 11:20–30

#59..........Luke 7:36–50

WEEK 5, DAY 1 TIME: 20 MINUTES

#60 ....Luke 8:1–3

#61..........Matt 12:22–37; Mark 3:20–30

#62..........Matt 12:38–45

#63..........Matt 12:46–50; Mark 3:31–35; Luke 8:19–21

#64a ....Matt 13:1–23; Mark 4:1–20; Luke 8:4–15

WEEK 5, DAY 2 TIME: 17 MINUTES

#64b ....Matt 13:24–53; Mark 4:21–34; Luke 8:16–18

#65..........Matt 8:18, 23–27; Mark 4:35–41; Luke 8:22–25
(for Matt 8:19–22, see #93)

#66..........Matt 8:28–34; Mark 5:1–20; Luke 8:26–39

WEEK 5, DAY 3 TIME: 14 MINUTES

#67..........Matt 9:18–26; Mark 5:21–43; Luke 8:40–56

#68..........Matt 9:27–34

#69..........Matt 13:54–58; Mark 6:1–6a

WEEK 5, DAY 4 TIME: 14 MINUTES

#70..........Matt 9:35–11:1; Mark 6:6b–13; Luke 9:1–6

#71..........Matt 14:1–12; Mark 6:14–29; Luke 9:7–9

Later Galilean Ministry
April–October A.D. 29

LESSON 9 (#72–95) 1 HOUR, 11 MINUTES

WEEK 6, DAY 1 TIME: 20 MINUTES

#72..........Matt 14:13–21; Mark 6:30–44; Luke 9:10–17; John 6:1–13

#73–75.......Matt 14:22–36; Mark 6:45–56; John 6:14–21

#76..........John 6:22–71

WEEK 6, DAY 2 TIME: 18 MINUTES

#77..........Matt 15:1–20; Mark 7:1–23; John 7:1

#78..........Matt 15:21–28; Mark 7:24–30

#79..........Matt 15:29–38; Mark 7:31–8:9

#80–81 ......Matt 15:39–16:12; Mark 8:10–26

WEEK 6, DAY 3 TIME: 13 MINUTES

#82–84 . . . . . . Matt 16:13–28; Mark 8:27–9:1; Luke 9:18–27

#85–86 . . . . . . Matt 17:1–13; Mark 9:2–13; Luke 9:28–36

WEEK 6, DAY 4 TIME: 20 MINUTES

#87–88 . . . . . . Matt 17:14–23; Mark 9:14–32; Luke 9:37–45

#89. . . . . Matt 17:24–27

#90–92 . . . . . . Mark 9:33–50; Luke 9:46–50; Matt 18:1–35

#94–95 . . . . . . Luke 9:51–56; John 7:2–10

#93. . . . . Matt 8:19–22; Luke 9:57–62

LESSON 10 (#96–111) 56 MINUTES

Later Judean Ministry
October A.D. 28–December A.D. 29

WEEK 7, DAY 1 TIME: 16 MINUTES

#96. . . . . John 7:11–52

#97. . . . . John 7:53–8:11

#98. . . . . John 8:12–20

#99. . . . . John 8:21–59

WEEK 7, DAY 2 TIME: 16 MINUTES

#102 . . . . Luke 10:1–24

#103 . . . . Luke 10:25–37

#104. . . . . Luke 10:38–42

#105 . . . . Luke 11:1–13

#106. . . . . Luke 11:14–36

#107 . . . . Luke 11:37–54

WEEK 7, DAY 3 TIME: 13 MINUTES

#108.........Luke 12:1–59

#109.........Luke 13:1–9

#110 ....Luke 13:10–21

WEEK 7, DAY 4 TIME: 11 MINUTES

#100.........John 9:1–41
(see the Thomas and Gundry *NIV Harmony*, page 134, note "o" on the rearragement of #100–101)

#101 ....John 10:1–21

#111..........John 10:22–39

Perean Ministry
January–March A.D. 30

LESSON 11 (#112–127) 1 HOUR, 8 MINUTES

WEEK 8, DAY 1 TIME: 15 MINUTES

#112 ....John 10:40–42

#113 ....Luke 13:22–35

#114 ....Luke 14:1–24

#115 ....Luke 14:25–35

#116 ....Luke 15:1–32

WEEK 8, DAY 2 TIME: 14 MINUTES

#117 ....Luke 16:1–17:10

#120.........Luke 17:11–37

#121 ....Luke 18:1–14

WEEK 8, DAY 3 TIME: 8 MINUTES

#118 ....John 11:1–44

#119 ....John 11:45–54

WEEK 8, DAY 4 TIME: 16 MINUTES

#122.........Matt 19:1–12; Mark 10:1–12

#123 . . . . .Matt 19:13–15; Mark 10:13–16;
Luke 18:15–17

#124. . . . . .Matt 19:16–20:16; Mark 10:17–31;
Luke 18:18–30

WEEK 8, DAY 5 TIME: 15 MINUTES

#125 . . . . .Matt 20:17–28; Mark 10:32–45;
Luke 18:31–34

#126. . . . . .Matt 20:29–34; Mark 10:46–52;
Luke 18:35–43

#127 . . . . .Luke 19:1–27

LESSON 12 (#128–152) 2 HOURS, 9 MINUTES

The Final Week
March 31–April 6, A.D. 30

WEEK 9, DAY 1 TIME: 20 MINUTES

#128a . . . . .John 11:55–12:1, 9–11

#128b–131 . . . .Matt 21:1–22; Mark 11:1–26;
Luke 19:28–48; John 12:12–50

WEEK 9, DAY 2 TIME: 20 MINUTES

#132–134 . . . . .Matt 21:23–22:33; Mark 11:27–12:27;
Luke 20:1–40

WEEK 9, DAY 3 TIME: 13 MINUTES

#135–136 . . . . .Matt 22:34–46; Mark 12:28–37;
Luke 20:41–44

#137–138 . . . . .Matt 23:1–44; Mark 12:38–40;
Luke 20:45–21:4

WEEK 10, DAY 1 TIME: 14 MINUTES

#139 . . . . .Matt 24–25

WEEK 10, DAY 2 TIME: 11 MINUTES

#139 . . . . Mark 13:1–37; Luke 21:5–36

WEEK 10, DAY 3 TIME: 8 MINUTES

#140–142 . . . . Matt 26:1–16; Mark 14:1–11; Luke 22:1–6

WEEK 11, DAY 1 TIME: 18 MINUTES

#143–148. . . . . Matt 26:17–35; Mark 14:12–25; Luke 22:7–38; John 13:21–38; 1 Cor 11:23–26

WEEK 11, DAY 2 TIME: 15 MINUTES

#149–150. . . . . John 14–16

WEEK 11, DAY 3 TIME: 10 MINUTES

#151 . . . . John 17

#152 . . . . John 18:1; Matt 26:30, 36–46; Mark 14:26, 32–42; Luke 22:39–46

Jesus on Trial
April 7, A.D. 30

LESSON 13 (#153–161) 37 MINUTES

WEEK 12, DAY 1 TIME: 6 MINUTES

#153 . . . . Matt 26:47–56; Mark 14:43–52; Luke 22:47–53; John 18:2–11

WEEK 12, DAY 2 TIME: 17 MINUTES

154–158 . . . . . . Matt 26:57–27:10; Acts 1:18–19; Mark 14:53–15:1a; Luke 22:54–71; John 18:12–27

WEEK 12, DAY 3 TIME: 14 MINUTES

#159 . . . . Matt 27:2, 11–14; Mark 15:1b–5; Luke 23:1–5; John 18:28–38

#160.........Luke 23:6–12

#161 ....Matt 27:15–26; Mark 15:6–15;
Luke 23:13–25; John 18:39–19:16a

LESSON 14 (#162–168) 24 MINUTES

Crucifixion
April 7, A.D. 30

WEEK 12, DAY 4 TIME: 11 MINUTES

#162–164.....Matt 27:27–44; Mark 15:16–32;
Luke 23:26–43; John 19:16b–27

WEEK 12, DAY 5 TIME: 13 MINUTES

#165–168.....Matt 27:45–66; Mark 15:33–47;
Luke 23:44–56; John 19:28–42

LESSON 15 (#169–184) 29 MINUTES

The Resurrection
March 31–April 6, A.D. 30

WEEK 13, DAY 1 TIME: 11 MINUTES

#169–172.....Matt 28:1–8; Mark 16:1–8;
Luke 24:1–12; John 20:1–10

#173 ....Mark 16:9–11; John 20:11–18

#174–175 .....Matt 28:9–15

WEEK 13, DAY 2 TIME: 12 MINUTES

#176–179.....Mark 16:12–14; Luke 24:13–43;
John 20:19–31; 1 Cor 15:5

#180.........John 21:1–25

WEEK 13, DAY 3 TIME: 6 MINUTES

#181–182 .....Matt 28:16–20; Mark 16:15–18;
1 Cor 15:6–7

#183 ....Luke 24:44–49; Acts 1:3–8

#184.........Mark 16:19–20; Luke 24:50–53;
Acts 1:9–12

INDEX OF PASSAGES IN THE *HARMONY*